Law Firm Marketing

Law Firm Marketing

How to Promote Your Law Firm
Without Looking Like an Ambulance Chaser

By Chris Gattis & Felica Sparks

Published by Blue Point Publishers, a division of Blue Point Strategies, LLC, Huntsville, Alabama.

For information on discounts for bulk purchases and our other products, please contact Blue Point Publishers at
books@bluepointstrategies.com.

Chris Gattis cover picture by Melissa Tash Studios, Huntsville, Alabama.
Felica Sparks cover picture by Craig Shamwell Photography, Huntsville,
Alabama.

ISBN-13: 978-1468147339
ISBN-10: 1468147331

Printed in the United States of America

Limit of Liability/Disclaimer of Warranty

While the publisher and authors have used their best efforts in preparing this book, they make no representation or warranties with respect to the accuracy or completeness of the contents of this book and specifically disclaim any implied warranties of merchantability or fitness for a particular purpose. No warranty may be created or extended by sales representatives or written sales materials. The advice and strategies contained herein may not be suitable for your situation. You should consult with a professional when appropriate. Neither the publisher nor authors shall be liable for any loss of profit or any other commercial damages, including but not limited to special, incidental, consequential, or other damages.

Acknowledgements

A good story is only as good as a good editor. The authors wish to thank **Catherine Hamrick** at **911WriterEditor** for her excellent editing skills. Thanks to a special collaboration with Catherine, the entire business start-up series has a more professional polish.

A book is only as good as its cover! Thanks to **Mark Hogan** at **Primer Design Studios** for his design and layout skills on the book cover. Nice work, Mark!

Table of Contents

Introduction

You are an attorney. You have a law practice either by yourself, with a couple of associates, or in a large firm. You want more clients. But most attorneys who advertise on TV come across like Vinny Gambini trying to put together a class action for "utes" who play too many video games. What's a respectable lawyer to do?

The good news is you can promote your law practice and yourself while doing it in a way that supports the image you've been trying so hard to create. You can set yourself apart from other attorneys in your market while continuing to improve your reputation.

Creating a marketing plan for lawyers or other professionals is no different than creating a marketing plan for any other business. It starts with understanding your market, identifying your target customer, creating a marketing plan, and developing tactics to further your plan. In the end, you're trying to promote yourself and your business and bring in more customers.

Let's set some expectations about attorney advertising and professional ethics rules. We're not attorneys. We don't pretend that we know the advertising and ethics rules in the 50 states, related territories, or foreign countries. We have looked specifically at the Alabama Rules of Professional Conduct and the Model Rules of Professional Conduct. The next chapter will deal with the Model Rules and some of the

1

differences between the Model Rules and the Alabama Rules. Why Alabama? Because we live and work and consult primarily with attorney's in Alabama. This guide is written to agree with the Model Rules. We'll point out a couple of differences that apply to Alabama. If you're a practicing attorney, you should already understand the ethics rules in your state. If your state rules differ from the Model Rules, then adjust your behavior accordingly. If you are unsure of how your state's ethics rules apply in a particular situation, contact a knowledgeable associate in your state or your state bar association for assistance.

The main object of this book is to get you thinking about the process of creating a marketing plan and to suggest some common tactics for you to use, or not, depending on what you're trying to accomplish. All of the specific tactics mentioned in the two tactics chapters are just suggestions of tactics. You'll have to pick the specific tactics that work for your situation, your target customer, and your firm brand identity.

We don't think you need to know anything more about advertising ethics than you probably already know to begin developing a marketing plan. If you bought this book based on the title and you develop a plan following the steps outlined in it, using your own reputation as a barometer, your outcome should work out. We're not going to recommend loud and obnoxious marketing tactics in the first place. We're going to recommend using your own personality and reputation to build a plan that fits within your personal or firm brand. If you stay true to your brand and not make any ridiculous claims, you'll likely stay clear of ethics issues.

Your real issue with the ethics rules will come into play with your tactics. The advertising you run, the workshop you give, and how your business cards and letterhead are worded. This is where knowing the rules for your state is critical. Again, if you're a practicing attorney, you should be fully aware of the rules in your state. You can go to the American Bar Association (www.americanbar.org) to view the model rules, the differences between the model rules and your state and more discussion than you can read in a reasonable amount of time on the subject.

For most small businesses, marketing is some sort of "black magic" that isn't really understood. Most hopeful entrepreneurs, and especially lawyers, think they don't understand marketing at all. I'm not suggesting that developing a creative marketing plan is simple. But it's more about doing your research and laying out a logical plan based on that research than it is "black magic" wizardry.

Keep in mind that you'll develop a separate plan for each market segment. You'll need to approach each segment and target clients with a unique strategy. You should assume that all parts will be different for each market segment. After you get all the pieces laid out, you can combine and overlap where it makes sense to take best advantage of your available budget.

We like to approach developing a marketing plan as we would develop a business plan. Do your market research first, and then develop strategies based on customers and preferences. Consider the financial implications and launch. Use the template; adopt the steps to your business and market; develop the strategy and action plans; and put your plan into action. The businesses are different, the services are different, the people are different, but the steps required to develop the plan are essentially the same. This plan has been developed specifically to make it as easy as possible to develop a creative and effective plan for marketing a law practice. Just follow the steps, and you'll have good results.

Before we go any further, let's get some definitions under our belt. The following terms are used in this book to describe markets, functions, and tools used in marketing generally and in marketing for attorneys specifically.

Market Analysis: This is a brief restatement of the market conditions, trends, and major opportunities and threats.

Market Segments: Market segments define the different subgroups within an industry. For example, within the legal industry, there are market segments for corporate law, elder law, criminal defense, and so forth. In many cases, each of these segments will also have sub segments. As a marketer, you will be looking to certain segments and sub segments in which to do business. You will not do business in every segment in your industry. You will be developing a specific marketing plan for each of these target segments, or markets.

Target Customer: Target customers are your most likely customers. It's a group of potential customers with similar interests, needs, likes, or demographic makeup. These are the people or businesses that you think will most likely want your services. The needs and wants of this group are what you will build your marketing plan around.

Unique Sales Proposition: This is sometimes called a unique value proposition. Why would your target customer hire you instead of the firm down the street offering the same service? It's a statement of idea that sets you apart from your competition. In other words, why is your firm so special? Remember, it's all about the customer.

Marketing Strategy: Your marketing strategy is a plan that will be defined in terms of the 4 P's of marketing: product, price, place, and promotion.

Product: Your product is actually a service. What services will you promote to this target customer and how will the customer use them? How does your service solve the target customer's problem or make his or her life better? These questions will help you define your service offerings to your target customer. You will concentrate your service offerings based on the wants and needs of your target customer.

Price: Will you price higher or lower than your competition? What are the advantages of your pricing strategy relative to your brand and service level? Include list price, discounts, payment terms, and any other financial terms, such as leasing or financing options. This category usually seems obvious, but you need to make a conscious decision to price in a particular way.

Place: How will you get your service to the customer? The distribution channel you use will have a major impact on the pricing and promotion of the service. Will you use one channel exclusively (i.e. retail, direct, distribution, or manufacturer's rep) or some combination? Most attorneys use the "come to my office" distribution model. Is that exclusively right for your target customer?

Promotion: The promotion plan will be defined by outlining your goals or market objectives, budget, timetable, and resources necessary to implement the promotion of your services and your firm.

Goals (Market Objectives): Goals can be defined as selling a certain dollar amount or number of services or commanding a certain percentage of the total market. In some cases, as a law firm, you'll be trying to raise awareness of your firm and your capabilities. In these cases, you will not have a hard dollar or percentage increase but an awareness increase. Be careful of this type of goal because it is very difficult to measure.

Budget: The budget is the amount of money set aside for individual pieces of the marketing plan or the plan as a whole. Don't forget to include any R&D that might be necessary to get a service ready for market.

Timetable: The timetable is the amount of time needed to accomplish the goals of your marketing plan or individual tactic.

Resources Needed: What resources are necessary to meet your goals? You have already defined the cash requirement for the tactic, but what about employees, research costs, accounting, graphic art, web page, and other expenses?

Action Plan/Implementation Tactics: What, specifically, are you going to do? You'll be defining the specific implementation tactics necessary to promote your services.

Advertising and Promotion: How will you advertise your services? Will you use media, such as TV, radio, newspapers, magazines, trade journals, and billboards? Or will you use Internet marketing, e-mail campaigns, or pay-per-click advertising?

PR Campaigns: Will you use news conferences, YouTube videos, press releases, and industry website news to promote your services and/or company launch? There are many different definitions of advertising and PR. For our purposes here, we'll use this simple definition: advertising is bought; PR is free.

Networking: Networking can take the form of chamber of commerce "after hours" or breakfast events or a more formal networking such as Business Networking International (BNI). While many of these options do not have a direct cost, they do take time, something which may be in shorter supply than actual cash money.

Monitor/Measure/Test: One of the most important pieces of your marketing plan is the measurement. If you have set goals and objectives for your plans, you'll be able to measure the results. If you aren't getting the results you wanted, make changes to your plan. Describe how you will monitor the plans and measure your results.

Model Rules of Professional Conduct

As stated in the Introduction, we're not lawyers and we don't pretend to understand the rules of professional conduct for your state the way you should. Before putting your tactical plan into action, double check the rules in your state to make sure you are meeting the requirements. Notwithstanding any issues of client confidentiality and other normal professional conduct issues, the following is a listing with comments of the 7.0 series rules from the model code. These are the rules that apply specifically to marketing and advertising. Obviously, you need to follow the rules for your state.

The Model Rules of Professional Conduct (MRPC) listed here are as published on the American Bar Association's website as of March 2012. Since we work primarily with attorneys in Alabama, we've noted the differences between the Model Rules and the Alabama Rules of Professional Conduct (ARPC).

MRPC - Rule 7.1 Communications Concerning A Lawyer's Services

A lawyer shall not make a false or misleading communication about the lawyer or the lawyer's services. A communication is false or misleading if it contains a material misrepresentation of fact or law, or omits a fact necessary to make the statement considered as a whole not materially misleading.

Comment

[1] This Rule governs all communications about a lawyer's services, including advertising permitted by Rule 7.2. Whatever means are used to make known a lawyer's services, statements about them must be truthful.

[2] Truthful statements that are misleading are also prohibited by this Rule. A truthful statement is misleading if it omits a fact necessary to make the lawyer's communication considered as a whole not materially misleading. A truthful statement is also misleading if there is a substantial likelihood that it will lead a reasonable person to formulate a specific conclusion about the lawyer or the lawyer's services for which there is no reasonable factual foundation.

[3] An advertisement that truthfully reports a lawyer's achievements on behalf of clients or former clients may be misleading if presented so as to lead a reasonable person to form an unjustified expectation that the same results could be obtained for other clients in similar matters without reference to the specific factual and legal circumstances of each client's case. Similarly, an unsubstantiated comparison of the lawyer's services or fees with the services or fees of other lawyers may be misleading if presented with such specificity as would lead a reasonable person to conclude that the comparison can be substantiated. The inclusion of an appropriate disclaimer or qualifying language may preclude a finding that a statement

is likely to create unjustified expectations or otherwise mislead a prospective client.

[4] See also Rule 8.4(e) for the prohibition against stating or implying an ability to influence improperly a government agency or official or to achieve results by means that violate the Rules of Professional Conduct or other law.

ARPC - The Alabama rules are substantially the same as the model rules for Rule 7.1.

MRPC - Rule 7.2 Advertising

(a) Subject to the requirements of Rules 7.1 and 7.3, a lawyer may advertise services through written, recorded or electronic communication, including public media.

(b) A lawyer shall not give anything of value to a person for recommending the lawyer's services except that a lawyer may

(1) pay the reasonable costs of advertisements or communications permitted by this Rule;

(2) pay the usual charges of a legal service plan or a not-for-profit or qualified lawyer referral service. A qualified lawyer referral service is a lawyer referral service that has been approved by an appropriate regulatory authority;

(3) pay for a law practice in accordance with Rule 1.17; and

(4) refer clients to another lawyer or a nonlawyer professional pursuant to an agreement not otherwise prohibited under these Rules that provides for the other person to refer clients or customers to the lawyer, if

(i) the reciprocal referral agreement is not exclusive, and

(ii) the client is informed of the existence and nature of the agreement.

(c) Any communication made pursuant to this rule shall include the name and office address of at least one lawyer or law firm responsible for its content.

Comment

[1] To assist the public in obtaining legal services, lawyers should be allowed to make known their services not only through reputation but also through organized information campaigns in the form of advertising. Advertising involves an active quest for clients, contrary to the tradition that a lawyer should not seek clientele. However, the public's need to know about legal services can be fulfilled in part through advertising. This need is particularly acute in the case of persons of moderate means who have not made extensive use of legal services. The interest in expanding public information about legal services ought to prevail over considerations of tradition. Nevertheless, advertising by lawyers entails the risk of practices that are misleading or overreaching.

[2] This Rule permits public dissemination of information concerning a lawyer's name or firm name, address and telephone number; the kinds of services the lawyer will undertake; the basis on which the lawyer's fees are determined, including prices for specific services and payment and credit arrangements; a lawyer's foreign language ability; names of references and, with their consent, names of clients regularly represented; and other information that might invite the attention of those seeking legal assistance.

[3] Questions of effectiveness and taste in advertising are matters of speculation and subjective judgment. Some jurisdictions have had extensive prohibitions against television advertising, against advertising going beyond specified facts about a lawyer, or against "undignified" advertising. Television is now one of the most powerful media for getting information to the public, particularly persons of low and moderate income; prohibiting television advertising,

therefore, would impede the flow of information about legal services to many sectors of the public. Limiting the information that may be advertised has a similar effect and assumes that the bar can accurately forecast the kind of information that the public would regard as relevant. Similarly, electronic media, such as the Internet, can be an important source of information about legal services, and lawful communication by electronic mail is permitted by this Rule. But see Rule 7.3(a) for the prohibition against the solicitation of a prospective client through a real-time electronic exchange that is not initiated by the prospective client.

[4] Neither this Rule nor Rule 7.3 prohibits communications authorized by law, such as notice to members of a class in class action litigation.

Paying Others to Recommend a Lawyer

[5] Lawyers are not permitted to pay others for channeling professional work. Paragraph (b)(1), however, allows a lawyer to pay for advertising and communications permitted by this Rule, including the costs of print directory listings, on-line directory listings, newspaper ads, television and radio airtime, domain-name registrations, sponsorship fees, banner ads, and group advertising. A lawyer may compensate employees, agents and vendors who are engaged to provide marketing or client-development services, such as publicists, public-relations personnel, business-development staff and website designers. See Rule 5.3 for the duties of lawyers and law firms with respect to the conduct of nonlawyers who prepare marketing materials for them.

[6] A lawyer may pay the usual charges of a legal service plan or a not-for-profit or qualified lawyer referral service. A legal service plan is a prepaid or group legal service plan or a similar delivery system that assists prospective clients to secure legal representation. A lawyer referral service, on the

13

other hand, is any organization that holds itself out to the public as a lawyer referral service. Such referral services are understood by laypersons to be consumer-oriented organizations that provide unbiased referrals to lawyers with appropriate experience in the subject matter of the representation and afford other client protections, such as complaint procedures or malpractice insurance requirements. Consequently, this Rule only permits a lawyer to pay the usual charges of a not-for-profit or qualified lawyer referral service. A qualified lawyer referral service is one that is approved by an appropriate regulatory authority as affording adequate protections for prospective clients. See, e.g., the American Bar Association's Model Supreme Court Rules Governing Lawyer Referral Services and Model Lawyer Referral and Information Service Quality Assurance Act (requiring that organizations that are identified as lawyer referral services (i) permit the participation of all lawyers who are licensed and eligible to practice in the jurisdiction and who meet reasonable objective eligibility requirements as may be established by the referral service for the protection of prospective clients; (ii) require each participating lawyer to carry reasonably adequate malpractice insurance; (iii) act reasonably to assess client satisfaction and address client complaints; and (iv) do not refer prospective clients to lawyers who own, operate or are employed by the referral service.)

[7] A lawyer who accepts assignments or referrals from a legal service plan or referrals from a lawyer referral service must act reasonably to assure that the activities of the plan or service are compatible with the lawyer's professional obligations. See Rule 5.3. Legal service plans and lawyer referral services may communicate with prospective clients, but such communication must be in conformity with these Rules. Thus, advertising must not be false or misleading, as would be the case if the communications of a group advertising program or a group legal services plan would

mislead prospective clients to think that it was a lawyer referral service sponsored by a state agency or bar association. Nor could the lawyer allow in-person, telephonic, or real-time contacts that would violate Rule 7.3.

[8] A lawyer also may agree to refer clients to another lawyer or a nonlawyer professional, in return for the undertaking of that person to refer clients or customers to the lawyer. Such reciprocal referral arrangements must not interfere with the lawyer's professional judgment as to making referrals or as to providing substantive legal services. See Rules 2.1 and 5.4(c). Except as provided in Rule 1.5(e), a lawyer who receives referrals from a lawyer or nonlawyer professional must not pay anything solely for the referral, but the lawyer does not violate paragraph (b) of this Rule by agreeing to refer clients to the other lawyer or nonlawyer professional, so long as the reciprocal referral agreement is not exclusive and the client is informed of the referral agreement. Conflicts of interest created by such arrangements are governed by Rule 1.7. Reciprocal referral agreements should not be of indefinite duration and should be reviewed periodically to determine whether they comply with these Rules. This Rule does not restrict referrals or divisions of revenues or net income among lawyers within firms comprised of multiple entities.

ARPC – The Alabama rules allow most forms of advertising; print, media, outdoor, internet, and private on-line service. The ARPC requires that advertisements be delivered to the State Bar within three days of their first being shown to the public, along with detailed information about publisher and ad duration. Additionally, the ARPC requires that copies of ads be maintained in the attorney's office for six years, not two years as required in the MRPC. Attorneys are not allowed to advertise special rates just to generate new business, are required to hold advertised rates for 60 days, and requires special language to accompany any advertisement.

Rule 7.3 Direct Contact With Prospective Clients

(a) A lawyer shall not by in-person, live telephone or real-time electronic contact solicit professional employment from a prospective client when a significant motive for the lawyer's doing so is the lawyer's pecuniary gain, unless the person contacted:

(1) is a lawyer; or

(2) has a family, close personal, or prior professional relationship with the lawyer.

(b) A lawyer shall not solicit professional employment from a prospective client by written, recorded or electronic communication or by in-person, telephone or real-time electronic contact even when not otherwise prohibited by paragraph (a), if:

(1) the prospective client has made known to the lawyer a desire not to be solicited by the lawyer; or

(2) the solicitation involves coercion, duress or harassment.

(c) Every written, recorded or electronic communication from a lawyer soliciting professional employment from a prospective client known to be in need of legal services in a particular matter shall include the words "Advertising Material" on the outside envelope, if any, and at the beginning and ending of any recorded or electronic communication, unless the recipient of the communication is a person specified in paragraphs (a)(1) or (a)(2).

(d) Notwithstanding the prohibitions in paragraph (a), a lawyer may participate with a prepaid or group legal service plan operated by an organization not owned or directed by the lawyer that uses in-person or telephone contact to solicit memberships or subscriptions for the plan from persons who are not known to need legal services in a particular matter covered by the plan.

Comment

[1] There is a potential for abuse inherent in direct in-person, live telephone or real-time electronic contact by a lawyer with a prospective client known to need legal services. These forms of contact between a lawyer and a prospective client subject the layperson to the private importuning of the trained advocate in a direct interpersonal encounter. The prospective client, who may already feel overwhelmed by the circumstances giving rise to the need for legal services, may find it difficult fully to evaluate all available alternatives with reasoned judgment and appropriate self-interest in the face of the lawyer's presence and insistence upon being retained immediately. The situation is fraught with the possibility of undue influence, intimidation, and over-reaching.

[2] This potential for abuse inherent in direct in-person, live telephone or real-time electronic solicitation of prospective clients justifies its prohibition, particularly since lawyer advertising and written and recorded communication permitted under Rule 7.2 offer alternative means of conveying necessary information to those who may be in need of legal services. Advertising and written and recorded communications which may be mailed or autodialed make it possible for a prospective client to be informed about the need for legal services, and about the qualifications of available lawyers and law firms, without subjecting the prospective client to direct in-person, telephone or real-time electronic persuasion that may overwhelm the client's judgment.

[3] The use of general advertising and written, recorded or electronic communications to transmit information from lawyer to prospective client, rather than direct in-person, live telephone or real-time electronic contact, will help to assure that the information flows cleanly as well as freely. The

17

contents of advertisements and communications permitted under Rule 7.2 can be permanently recorded so that they cannot be disputed and may be shared with others who know the lawyer. This potential for informal review is itself likely to help guard against statements and claims that might constitute false and misleading communications, in violation of Rule 7.1. The contents of direct in-person, live telephone or real-time electronic conversations between a lawyer and a prospective client can be disputed and may not be subject to third-party scrutiny. Consequently, they are much more likely to approach (and occasionally cross) the dividing line between accurate representations and those that are false and misleading.

[4] There is far less likelihood that a lawyer would engage in abusive practices against an individual who is a former client, or with whom the lawyer has close personal or family relationship, or in situations in which the lawyer is motivated by considerations other than the lawyer's pecuniary gain. Nor is there a serious potential for abuse when the person contacted is a lawyer. Consequently, the general prohibition in Rule 7.3(a) and the requirements of Rule 7.3(c) are not applicable in those situations. Also, paragraph (a) is not intended to prohibit a lawyer from participating in constitutionally protected activities of public or charitable legal- service organizations or bona fide political, social, civic, fraternal, employee or trade organizations whose purposes include providing or recommending legal services to its members or beneficiaries.

[5] But even permitted forms of solicitation can be abused. Thus, any solicitation which contains information which is false or misleading within the meaning of Rule 7.1, which involves coercion, duress or harassment within the meaning of Rule 7.3(b)(2), or which involves contact with a prospective client who has made known to the lawyer a desire not to be solicited by the lawyer within the meaning of Rule 7.3(b)(1) is

prohibited. Moreover, if after sending a letter or other communication to a client as permitted by Rule 7.2 the lawyer receives no response, any further effort to communicate with the prospective client may violate the provisions of Rule 7.3(b).

[6] This Rule is not intended to prohibit a lawyer from contacting representatives of organizations or groups that may be interested in establishing a group or prepaid legal plan for their members, insureds, beneficiaries or other third parties for the purpose of informing such entities of the availability of and details concerning the plan or arrangement which the lawyer or lawyer's firm is willing to offer. This form of communication is not directed to a prospective client. Rather, it is usually addressed to an individual acting in a fiduciary capacity seeking a supplier of legal services for others who may, if they choose, become prospective clients of the lawyer. Under these circumstances, the activity which the lawyer undertakes in communicating with such representatives and the type of information transmitted to the individual are functionally similar to and serve the same purpose as advertising permitted under Rule 7.2.

[7] The requirement in Rule 7.3(c) that certain communications be marked "Advertising Material" does not apply to communications sent in response to requests of potential clients or their spokespersons or sponsors. General announcements by lawyers, including changes in personnel or office location, do not constitute communications soliciting professional employment from a client known to be in need of legal services within the meaning of this Rule.

[8] Paragraph (d) of this Rule permits a lawyer to participate with an organization which uses personal contact to solicit members for its group or prepaid legal service plan, provided that the personal contact is not undertaken by any lawyer who would be a provider of legal services through the plan. The

organization must not be owned by or directed (whether as manager or otherwise) by any lawyer or law firm that participates in the plan. For example, paragraph (d) would not permit a lawyer to create an organization controlled directly or indirectly by the lawyer and use the organization for the in-person or telephone solicitation of legal employment of the lawyer through memberships in the plan or otherwise. The communication permitted by these organizations also must not be directed to a person known to need legal services in a particular matter, but is to be designed to inform potential plan members generally of another means of affordable legal services. Lawyers who participate in a legal service plan must reasonably assure that the plan sponsors are in compliance with Rules 7.1, 7.2 and 7.3(b). See 8.4(a).

ARPC - The Alabama rules are substantially the same as the model rules for Rule 7.3.

Rule 7.4 Communication of Fields of Practice and Specialization

(a) A lawyer may communicate the fact that the lawyer does or does not practice in particular fields of law.

(b) A lawyer admitted to engage in patent practice before the United States Patent and Trademark Office may use the designation "Patent Attorney" or a substantially similar designation.

(c) A lawyer engaged in Admiralty practice may use the designation "Admiralty," "Proctor in Admiralty" or a substantially similar designation.

(d) A lawyer shall not state or imply that a lawyer is certified as a specialist in a particular field of law, unless:

(1) the lawyer has been certified as a specialist by an organization that has been approved by an appropriate state authority or that has been accredited by the American Bar Association; and

(2) the name of the certifying organization is clearly identified in the communication.

Comment

[1] Paragraph (a) of this Rule permits a lawyer to indicate areas of practice in communications about the lawyer's services. If a lawyer practices only in certain fields, or will not accept matters except in a specified field or fields, the lawyer is permitted to so indicate. A lawyer is generally permitted to state that the lawyer is a "specialist," practices a "specialty," or "specializes in" particular fields, but such communications are subject to the "false and misleading" standard applied in Rule 7.1 to communications concerning a lawyer's services.

[2] Paragraph (b) recognizes the long-established policy of the Patent and Trademark Office for the designation of lawyers practicing before the Office. Paragraph (c) recognizes that designation of Admiralty practice has a long historical tradition associated with maritime commerce and the federal courts.

[3] Paragraph (d) permits a lawyer to state that the lawyer is certified as a specialist in a field of law if such certification is granted by an organization approved by an appropriate state authority or accredited by the American Bar Association or another organization, such as a state bar association, that has been approved by the state authority to accredit organizations that certify lawyers as specialists. Certification signifies that an objective entity has recognized an advanced degree of knowledge and experience in the specialty area greater than is suggested by general licensure to practice law. Certifying organizations may be expected to apply standards of

experience, knowledge and proficiency to insure that a lawyer's recognition as a specialist is meaningful and reliable. In order to insure that consumers can obtain access to useful information about an organization granting certification, the name of the certifying organization must be included in any communication regarding the certification.

ARPC - The Alabama rules are substantially the same as the model rules for Rule 7.4 except they allow an attorney to communicate a specialist certification only if the organization granting the certification has prior approval by the Alabama State Bar Board of Legal Certification.

Rule 7.5 Firm Names And Letterheads

(a) A lawyer shall not use a firm name, letterhead or other professional designation that violates Rule 7.1. A trade name may be used by a lawyer in private practice if it does not imply a connection with a government agency or with a public or charitable legal services organization and is not otherwise in violation of Rule 7.1.

(b) A law firm with offices in more than one jurisdiction may use the same name or other professional designation in each jurisdiction, but identification of the lawyers in an office of the firm shall indicate the jurisdictional limitations on those not licensed to practice in the jurisdiction where the office is located.

(c) The name of a lawyer holding a public office shall not be used in the name of a law firm, or in communications on its behalf, during any substantial period in which the lawyer is not actively and regularly practicing with the firm.

(d) Lawyers may state or imply that they practice in a partnership or other organization only when that is the fact.

Comment

[1] A firm may be designated by the names of all or some of its members, by the names of deceased members where there has been a continuing succession in the firm's identity or by a trade name such as the "ABC Legal Clinic." A lawyer or law firm may also be designated by a distinctive website address or comparable professional designation. Although the United States Supreme Court has held that legislation may prohibit the use of trade names in professional practice, use of such names in law practice is acceptable so long as it is not misleading. If a private firm uses a trade name that includes a geographical name such as "Springfield Legal Clinic," an express disclaimer that it is a public legal aid agency may be required to avoid a misleading implication. It may be observed that any firm name including the name of a deceased partner is, strictly speaking, a trade name. The use of such names to designate law firms has proven a useful means of identification. However, it is misleading to use the name of a lawyer not associated with the firm or a predecessor of the firm, or the name of a nonlawyer.

[2] With regard to paragraph (d), lawyers sharing office facilities, but who are not in fact associated with each other in a law firm, may not denominate themselves as, for example, "Smith and Jones," for that title suggests that they are practicing law together in a firm.

ARPC - The Alabama rules are essentially the same as the model rules for Rule 7.5 with the addition of a provision that the name of a lawyer holding public office may not be used in the firm name or in communication of the firm name during any substantial period when the lawyer is not actually practicing with the firm.

Rule 7.6 Political Contributions To Obtain Legal Engagements Or Appointments By Judges

A lawyer or law firm shall not accept a government legal engagement or an appointment by a judge if the lawyer or law firm makes a political contribution or solicits political contributions for the purpose of obtaining or being considered for that type of legal engagement or appointment.

ARPC - Alabama did not adopt rule 7.6 from the Model Rules but instead created a new rule 7.6 entitled "Professional Cards for Nonlawyers" which prohibits the use of business cards by nonlawyers to be false or misleading. The intention being that the general public not mistake a nonlawyer employee of a law firm for an actual lawyer. A person with a title of "Legal Assistant" should be properly supervised by a lawyer.

Again, this is a listing of the Model Rules of Professional Conduct with our commentary on the differences for Alabama. You should check the rules in your state before putting your strategy into action.

Research Tools

In order to identify and understand your market, segments, competition, distribution channels, and customers, you're going to have to do some research. Even a seasoned industry pro will start by doing research. Where will you get the information that you need? There are many sources of information and in the age of the Internet, maybe in some cases, too many sources. Be careful where your research-produced information comes from. There are as many "experts" as there are websites with content. Just because someone wrote a blog entry about your profession does not mean that the information is factual or that the blogger is an expert. Anyone can create a website and pretend to be an expert. Some do this as a means of promoting a political position or a personal economic incentive. Keep in mind where your "data" comes from and make sure it's a source that you trust.

Understand that we're not talking about research for a legal cause or court case. We assume that you know the sources for practicing law. We're talking about market research—the sources you need to practice marketing.

Here is a listing of a few common sources of information:

Census Bureau: The Census Bureau has some excellent demographic information available from their website, http://factfinder.census.gov/. This information is free to the public and is available from any computer with an Internet connection. You can sort the information by state, county, city, or even zip code.

Public Library: The local public library has many sources of market data. Many larger libraries have extensive periodicals, from multifamily apartment construction to zoo management. Look through the magazines and journals to see whether they carry ones that might be interesting to your particular profession. They might have many years of old periodicals and newspapers on file. In addition, they will likely have technical and financial books relating to companies and industries that you can view in the reference section.

Many large libraries have a reference librarian whose job it is to help you find information that you need. If you are pleasant and courteous, he or she will normally bend over backwards to assist you in your search for information. If you explain that you are developing a marketing plan and trying to find some information about an industry, segment, or competitor, the reference librarian will give you some possible sources and might even do some searching for you.

Library cards are available for free to members of the community. If you live out of town, you might have to pay a small fee for a library card, which gives you the privilege to check out materials and use the library's on-line resources. Many libraries have subscriptions to on-line commercial databases that make your research easier and more convenient. You can generally access these resources through the library website from the comfort of your home or office.

Virtual Library: Virtual library cards are available for using the many sources of nonpublic information. These sources could be public policy institutes, research, or databases maintained by universities, public or private companies, and other research related sites. The information is generally only available to educational or research organizations and requires a special subscription. Many public libraries have these subscriptions and make them available to their patrons. This virtual library card can usually be used from your home computer by logging into the library's information portal. Just ask the library employees whether your local library offers a virtual library card.

University Library: Just like the public libraries, most university libraries are open for use by the local community. If you aren't sure, give them a call. For serious research about specific topics, university librarians are generally happy to assist. They're used to working with students and will gladly help business persons who approach them with a friendly attitude and gracious spirit.

Chamber of Commerce: Many local chambers of commerce have subscriptions to databases of census and geographic information services (GIS) that can be made available to their members. Many large chambers have staff available to assist in research for new company recruitment and member business expansion and large projects. If you are unsure, call your chamber and ask whether they can help.

Small Business Administration: The SBA has lots of resources for hopeful and existing entrepreneurs alike. Just visit the website www.sba.gov.

Paid Sources: For larger companies or big marketing campaigns, there are many different sources of paid industry content. Sources such as Hoover's, Dunn & Bradstreet, IBISWorld, and others offer industry specific information on the competitive landscape, demographics, trends, industry size, and critical issues that are updated on a regular basis. This information is available on a paid subscription basis. In addition, census data merged with consumer buying patterns and preferences are now available from several different companies. This information is relatively expensive, but it is used to be available only to the largest retail giants and consulting firms that can afford programming staff to generate the data. Many public or university libraries now offer access to this type data through their subscriptions. For large campaigns with high risk factors, this type data may be worth whatever the price.

Trade Associations: Most industries have a trade association that serves as the advocate for the industry. In many large industries, there may be several different groups serving similar needs for different segments of the industry. You may have to join the association to access their data, but they typically are an excellent source of specific and relevant information about your industry. If you don't find what you're looking for on their website, call the office and speak with a representative. Again, these individuals are generally more than willing to assist a potential new member to find the information that he or she is seeking.

Market Testing: If you need specific information about consumer buying habits, you probably need to do some market testing. Most people over the age of forty remember the Coke vs. Pepsi taste tests on TV. This "market testing" was actually a Pepsi commercial, but the idea behind the commercial was a valid market test for consumers taste preference in soft drinks. One upscale clothing chain conducted a nearly year-long market test to see how the color of their sales staff's suits affected the purchasing habits of their customers. Most law firms will not need this extensive preference testing, but if your potential service rollout is very large and costly, it might make sense to get some reliable consumer preference information. You can do this with focus groups, service testing, surveys, and interviews, among others. This type of research can be done by the owner, but unless you truly understand how this process works or have the time to research and study how to do it, it's better left to professionals. While this may be the most expensive type of market research you conduct, it may also be the most helpful.

Focus Groups: Focus groups are an important component of market research. This type of research can be conducted on a formal or informal basis. The type of study you use will depend on how much money you have budgeted and the size of the firm's launch of services. An informal focus group might include a one-on-one discussion with customers, employees, service vendors and firm management to gather information about your company and market perceptions. If your risk is high or you need exacting information about style or substance relating to branding or service presentation, you might need to conduct formal focus groups. A semiscientific method might be selecting individuals from a group of customers, service vendors, employees, and friends who meet specific demographic characteristics. It can give you a quick and inexpensive group on which to test your ideas. If the stakes or the risks are really high, you will probably want to hire a professional firm to conduct the group studies. If you don't know how to do this, get some help.

You should conduct some market behavior research as a part of your everyday business information gathering. How does the way your employees are dressed affect customer behavior? What about how you greet your customers on the phone or in person? To be effective, you must measure what you're doing and the results you get. The only way to get valuable information is to make changes to your system and measure the results compared to the results you got before the change. You may need to try several iterations before you hit on the best method or style. Data gathering in every part of your business is the only way to truly measure the variables in place and the results that were produced.

The Marketing Plan Template

This book will be laid out in sections. We'll give you the template first with details and explanations following. If you understand the template, you can whiz right through the process. If there's something you need a little help with, read the details.

The Marketing Plan Template is comprised of four steps: research, strategy, tactics, and metrics. All good marketing plans begin with research. The second step is developing a strategy followed by tactics or action plan. Finally, you need to monitor the results from your marketing plan to ensure that you get the exposure, sales, or other benefits you planned for in your strategy.

Market Research
    Industry
    Competition
    Customers
    Company

Marketing Strategy
    Unique Sales Proposition
    Brand
    Service
    Promotion Goals

Promotion Tactics

Advertising and Promotion
Public Relations
Networking
Action Plans

Metrics

This template system will allow you to break down your marketing plan activity into four steps: 1) market research, 2) marketing strategy, 3) promotion tactics, and 4) metrics. In the first step, you will conduct research on the industry, competition, customers, and your company. This is an important step not to be skipped. Step 2 involves determining how you will set your company apart from your competition, what your goals are, and how you'll do business based on the research you completed in Step 1. Step 3 involves developing action plans that will put your marketing goals into practice. This is where you'll buy advertising, network, and conduct social media marketing efforts, depending on what makes sense for your business. Step 4 involves comparing the results derived from the previous steps and making the necessary changes to your plan to maximize your results. You'll want to constantly tweak your plans to bring a continuous improvement philosophy to your marketing plan.

The actual action plans that you put into place will depend on your research and how you want to communicate with your target customers. The specific action plans, or tactics, will be different for every firm and service line. This is where you get to use your creativity to communicate your company values to the marketplace.

In the next three chapters, we'll outline and describe the first three steps involved in creating a marketing plan. Then we'll look at specific tactics for attorneys followed by a brief discussion of metrics. If you jump ahead to The Attorney Action Plan, don't forget to come back and work through the first steps. Starting at the end will result in a thrown together plan that doesn't address the concerns of your target customers and will most likely be ineffective.

Market Research

The first part of your plan, as we've said before, is the research portion. You'll want to break down your research into four categories: 1) industry and markets, 2) competition, 3) customers, and 4) company. The market analysis template follows:

Market Research

Industry
Description of Industry
Industry Trends
Market Segment(s)
Distribution Channels

Competition
Direct and Indirect Competition
Strengths and Weaknesses

Customers
Demographics

Company
Company Profile

Industry

Understanding your market is one of the important first steps in preparing to develop a marketing plan. An understanding of how your market works and the size and potential for either a new company or an expanded role for an existing company in the market structure is each a key component. Who are your competitors and why would a potential customer buy from you? Understanding the market is the most important part of the marketing process.

While this part seems to be simple and is often overlooked or skipped, it requires a serious analysis of each component. Brainstorm and research each market segment in which you will compete, and then boil down the results into a form to help you "see" the market at a glance. Once you've assembled all the information, list it in a matrix format to get an "at a glance" view of your market. You may also use the Market Matrix Worksheet that is available for download at **www.BusinessStart-up101.com**.

Some of the critical questions you need to answer are:

How big is the market?

In actual client billings, how much combined do all the participants in the market sell? This can be a little tricky if you're a litigator. The size of the market can be defined by the last large suit won or class action filed. Don't get hung up on that. Think about the kind of day-to-day business you and your firm practice. Can the market support another competitor? Knowing how big the market is and who has the major share will help you determine your strategy.

What percent of the market share do you want or need?

Based on your own financial projections, what percentage share of the market will your billings represent? Is that a reasonable percentage? If your financial projections show your company with a large percentage of the market share, do a reality check with your advisors or mentors to confirm your projections and assumptions.

If you are hoping to be a national market player, how will the large competitors in the market react to your entry into the market and subsequent rise from a small company that they can ignore to a real competitor?

What are the different market segments?

Most industries have many different segments that make up a market. For example, lawyers could practice in corporate law, personal law, elder law, criminal law, or intellectual property, just to name a few. Within each segment, there are subsegments. For example, within the corporate law segment, there are subsegments for corporate bankruptcy, real estate, mergers and acquisitions, collections, and contracts. Almost all industries have several to dozens of market segments and hundreds of subsegments and sub-subsegments.

In which market segments will your company compete?

Known as your target market, these are the primary market segments in which you will compete. If you practice corporate law, you are probably not concerned about representing individuals in a DUI arrest. Similarly, if your firm specializes in elder law, you probably will not practice in the intellectual property segment. The larger the firm, however, the broader the segments in which you will practice. For smaller firms, it can be a balancing act trying to offer a range of services that will meet the needs of your best customers without trying to meet every need they will ever have.

Many markets likely already have a dominant player or players who serve a broad section of the market, perhaps operating across many different segments. How will you compete with these dominant players? Perhaps you can find a niche segment or subsegment in which to operate. If you're not looking to awaken the sleeping giant, the major player in the market, perhaps your best bet is to think small. By that, we mean to operate within a small niche at first to prove your model and fine-tune your business skills. After you have smoothed out the rough spots in your operating model, only then might you want to expand your business to serve a larger segment.

Distribution Channels

Distribution channels are the way in which you'll get your services to your customers. This probably seems irrelevant for a lawyer, and for many of you, it probably is standard. Notice we didn't agree to the word irrelevant. It's not irrelevant at all.

Most attorneys do business by leasing a nice office, many times in a downtown or other centralized area, and hanging out a shingle. They wait for clients to call or walk in the front door. If they do, the attorneys counsel them in their offices and send them a bill for a retainer. The follow-up visits are on the phone or sometimes in person. Once a month or so, they send the clients a bill. Does that describe your distribution channel?

In most industries, how you go to market will be largely defined by your individual market. If everyone in the market uses the same distribution method and your target customers prefer that method, then you're probably limited to operating largely with that distribution method. That's not to say you can't offer your services through other channels, but be prepared to be underwhelmed by the response from your customers. However, business is an ever changing dynamic, and new models are designed and tested every day. Who's to say your new ideas about distribution channels aren't the next industry standard?

What is your distribution strategy? What channels will you use? How do the standard distribution channels affect the way you plan to do business? Do you need partners with capabilities? How can you improve the standard channels and business models to make it easier for your customers to do business with you versus your competition? What a novel approach for an attorney, focusing on making it easier for your customer to do business with your firm. Cutting edge businesses ask this question every day. When is the last time you asked it?

Do your research; know your customer preferences, and test your methods before investing lots of money in an untested method. Who would have guessed in 1990 that movies would be rented by downloading them directly from your TV or by making a selection from a red vending machine and not by driving to a retail store where you would browse the shelves in search of your favorite film in VHS format? Customer preferences change, technology escalates, and business models evolve. Keep an open mind to potential new ways of doing business. It doesn't matter whether you're a lawyer, baker, or candlestick maker; things change.

Competition

Determine who your direct and indirect competitors are in the target market you will serve. What's the difference between "direct" and "indirect" competition? Direct competitors offer the same type services as you and operate a similar business in the same market. Think about this business example. If you own a local diner serving breakfast and lunch to locals, your direct competition would be other small, quick-service restaurants, fast-food establishments, and maybe coffee shops and convenience stores. They all offer a quick meal at a low or reasonable price. For a law practice, it's the other law firms in town that practice in the same general areas as your firm.

Let's continue to use the food industry as an example. Your indirect competitors are grocery stores, fine dining establishments, and national companies that deliver frozen or specially packaged foods via mail or delivery service. These type companies all provide food, but it's not a quick, inexpensive breakfast or lunch meal. For a law firm, there are on-line legal services that offer consumers the ability to create their own legal documents and national firms without a physical presence in your town but with the ability to operate as if they were there.

Make a list of the direct competition within your geographic market. Understand how they do business, the types of products or services in which they specialize, and to the best of your ability, their strengths and weaknesses. That is, what do they do well and not so well?

I find it helpful—especially in markets where the location of the firm is an important factor in the consumers' decisions to buy or not buy—to mark each competitor's location on a map. This specific location reference can help you identify strengths and weaknesses that are geographical in nature and that might not be obvious at first. Pay attention to traffic counts and demographic patterns in the market.

Also make a list of your indirect competitors. Their presence and obvious strengths and weaknesses will help you identify niches in the market and develop strategies to leverage your strengths or your competitors' weaknesses.

Don't think for a moment that you don't have any competition. It's not true. You have competition. Even if there is a brand new market emerging, someone else can mobilize in reaction to it with more people and more money than you. That you've poured your heart and soul and probably your life savings into this venture is irrelevant. Your competition is in the business to make money, and you now represent a threat to them.

How will you differentiate yourself and your firm from every other firm in your market segment? This question is at the heart of your business model, your service offering, and your distribution channel. How will you do business better, smarter, cheaper, faster, or more responsively to customer needs than your competition? Be careful of going for the cheaper angle. Customers don't always respond to the cheapest price model in the ways you would expect. You have to carefully consider your market segment, what your competition is doing, and how they price and go to market, and then find your niche in an underserved segment.

Can you make money in this business? After looking at your direct and indirect competitors, now is a good time to look at their pricing compared to your pricing. How does your cost structure relate to the cost structure your competition uses? What are the advantages and disadvantages of pricing higher or lower than your competition?

Is it really an advantage to be the cheapest seller in the market? For many consumer products, Wal-Mart (or other big box stores) is the price leader. And against their revenues in the hundreds of billions of dollars through 8,000+ retail outlets, most companies could never compete with them on price. And would you really want to try? Having the lowest price may work against you, depending on your market. Will you be viewed as less competent if your competitors charge $285 per hour and you charge $165? If the difference in billing rates is simply a function of overhead, you may have a great selling point. Give your pricing model careful consideration, and don't pick any of those strategies haphazardly.

Customers

Who are your customers? Do you provide services for individuals or businesses? Try to break down your customer base into logical categories. If you sell to consumers, use demographic categories. The more precisely you can identify your customer base, whether individuals or other businesses, the more efficiently you can promote your business.

If you do business with individuals, or business-to-consumer (B2C), then identify the demographic categories that best describe your customers. Use any demographic category that makes sense for your business, such as age, sex, marital status, income, or education. There are many additional categories, such as home ownership, religious preference, school affiliation, and so forth. Use those categories that make sense for your service line and market.

In addition, identify where your customers live, work, play, eat, and worship. Also note what kind of vehicles they drive and anything else that is identifiable. We find that many times small firms don't really understand their customers. What about their income, age, or behavior makes your firm interesting to them? What about your services, mission, or corporate philosophy makes you more interesting to your potential customers than your competition?

Likewise, if you do business with other companies, or business-to-business (B2B), try to identify those characteristics that make your customer base identifiable. The more clearly you can identify your customers, the more accurate you can be when defining your marketing strategy.

Clearly define your target customers in the appropriate categories. Depending on your business, you may have defined an even more precise measurement system. If you have actual historical data from which to draw, use that information to get a better feel for your customers and their behaviors.

Company

Just as you looked closely at your competition to identify what they do well and not so well, you need to now turn the magnifying glass inward. Take a critical look at your own firm and how you operate in your market. One way we do this is with a tool called a SWOT analysis, which stands for strengths, weaknesses, opportunities, and threats.

SWOT Analysis

At this point in the process, you should have a good idea of the trends in your industry and within your specific market segment, as well as what your competitors do well and not so well. Additionally, you should understand what your customers need, want, and desire.

We'll now pull all this information together in the form of a SWOT analysis. The SWOT analysis is at the heart of the marketing process and will help you identify where opportunities in the market match strengths of your company. These intersections are sweet spots where your firm can take advantage of market opportunities with existing capital, employee knowledge, or technology. It will also help us identify where threats and weaknesses cross so you can make strategic plans to improve your firm's performance in these areas.

Management theory typically breaks down the SWOT analysis into internal and external environments, where strengths and weaknesses are internal to the firm, and where opportunities and threats are external to the market factors. While this breakdown makes sense in many instances, it can sometimes be confusing. (Are the strengths and weaknesses of your competition opportunities or threats?) What is important to understand is that the SWOT analysis will help you identify your resources and capabilities and how they match up against the other players in your market. It will identify what your firm is prepared to do better than your competition and what your customers expect if your operation is ill prepared to serve them.

The SWOT analysis begins to help you differentiate your firm from your competition and to help you successfully compete in a tough market.

Strengths

What are your organization's strengths?

Your strengths should be measured relative to your competition and the expectations of your customers. Following this internal-external theme, strengths are an internal analysis of how your company is prepared to compete in the market. A few examples of strengths are:

Technology: Strengths in technology might include practice management software, patents, proprietary databases, or special software.

Financial: Financial strengths might include a large cash reserve or untapped borrowing capability, low borrowing costs, or available investor base.

Geographic: Geographic strengths might include being ideally located in regard to suppliers, fabricators, or customers in a particular industry.

Employees: Perhaps your firm has a solid base of experienced and dedicated employees who provide excellent service to your customer base and support to your partners.

Strengths can come in many different forms, whether people, technology, brand, financial resources, or even strong customer loyalty.

Weaknesses

Like strengths, your weaknesses should be measured relative to your competition and customer expectations. In some cases, a weakness is the flip side of a strength. While an experienced staff may be a strength in providing customer support, it's also expensive to have a large and experienced staff. Also, having plenty of service capacity may be a strength, but it's also a weakness in that your employees aren't fully billable due to lack of work. Like strengths, the weaknesses analysis is a look inside your organization and how it's prepared to compete in the marketplace. Some examples of weaknesses are:

Technology: Technology weaknesses might include old customer management software that doesn't give you adequate capabilities, internal systems that aren't integrated, or systems with glitches.

Brand: Brand weaknesses include poor or no reputation in the market and a strong connection with a former attorney as you switch direction.

Financial: High cost of money, tapped out borrowing lines, no investors on hand, and high existing debt burden are examples of financial weaknesses.

Employees: Employee weaknesses include low employee morale, new and untrained employees in a high technology or complicated service line, and high absenteeism.

It's important to make an honest assessment of your position within the market. Kidding yourself will result in money spent on advertising and promotional efforts to the wrong market, wrong customers, or with the wrong service. These aforementioned categories are merely examples of possible weaknesses. Use any category or theme that is appropriate for your firm or your market.

Opportunities

What are your organization's opportunities?

With the opportunities analysis, we get to look outside the company at the market environment. How is your competition responding to the customers' needs? What niches are left unfilled or what services are unproduced or poorly done? Examples of opportunities are:

Legal/Regulatory: Opportunities in the legal and regulatory area include new environmental regulations with which your company is already compliant, new IRS rules that your accounting software is already configured to meet, or specialized training that your employees have already completed, allowing your firm to get out front in a particular compliance area.

Competition: Competition opportunities might include a major competitor exiting the market, consolidation within the market, or an emerging market in which no competition has yet to emerge.

Vertical Market: Perhaps a new vertical market develops where your company already has capabilities and trained legal staff at the ready.

Technology: New technology opportunities might exist from expansion of existing IT equipment or software patents owned by your company.

Contracts: Opportunities in demand might occur from major new contract appropriations, seasonal service demands, or trade barrier removal.

Threats

What are your organization's threats?

Like opportunities, threats come from the market, or external environment. Examples of threats are:

Political: Political or legislative changes in an industry might cause significant compliance issues.

Technology: Technology threats might include the requirement to utilize a new, expensive technology to comply with environmental requirements or possibly just an upgrade to your existing IT systems that will cause outages to service.

Substitution: Substitute organizations, such as on-line legal firms, might put significant cost pressures on your sales efforts.

Trends: Industry trends, like those facing the movie rental business, might force you to significantly change how you do business.

Changes to the external environment may provide opportunities to some and present threats to others. Depending on your own strengths and weaknesses, your firm may view these market changes differently than does your competition. Remember, these are just a few examples of the types of categories of strengths, weaknesses, opportunities, and threats your practice may face. Conduct brainstorming sessions with your leadership team. Compare your firm to the market in which you operate, the competition, the needs, and the wants of your customer base.

Analysis

It may be helpful to arrange the four categories in a simple grid. Draw a vertical and horizontal line across and through the middle of a sheet of paper or white board. Think of the left hand side of the grid as the internal environment, or your company. Think of the right hand side of the grid as the external environment, or your market. The top left box represents the strengths with the weaknesses on the bottom left. Opportunities are placed in the top right box with threats in the bottom right box.

SWOT Analysis Grid

Internal Environment	External Environment
Strengths	**Opportunities**
Weaknesses	**Threats**

As you study the top half of the box, you can compare your strengths with the opportunities in the market. Which strengths give you a natural advantage with which opportunities? Are any of the opportunities natural fits with your strengths?

Likewise, as you look at the threats in the marketplace, are there weaknesses that can be corrected to allow you to better leverage your company to fight? Maybe you were thinking of a new service line that now has significant threats because of industry trends that are just now being exposed by your research.

The SWOT analysis is a two-part exercise. Not only do you have to identify the items for the four categories, but then you must analyze how to move forward based on this information.

Where will you place operating priorities based on the competition, market forces, and your firm's ability to compete? This tool is a useful framework for making important strategic decisions about your direction and priorities.

Marketing Strategy

You've done all your research and think you're ready to start promoting your firm. How do you know you've got the service offering right? Like every other step in this process, you need a well-defined goal and plan to get you there. Outside of running out of cash, lacking a marketing plan is one of the leading causes of business failure. Having the right service, at the right price, in the right place, with the right promotion is a difficult balancing act.

Marketing Strategy

> Unique Sales Proposition
> Brand
> Service
> Promotion Goals

Unique Sales Proposition

What makes your firm so special? We touched on this idea earlier. If *you* don't know, how will your customers know? Hopefully, you have a very clear and organized way of thinking about how you are different from your competition. We call this your unique sales proposition (USP) or unique value proposition (UVP).

You probably decided to go into your particular type of law practice because you have an interest or background in one type of practice over another. Perhaps you identified an unfulfilled need, or you have technology or employee background in a particular area. Whatever your particular USP, you need to define it in a way that your customers can not only understand it but also embrace it.

Let's face it. Your customers do not care that you feel passionately about a particular cause or situation. They care only about what it means to them. If you feel strongly that you will do 10% of your caseload in pro bono work, what does that mean to them? Unless it means you'll have a cheaper price, quicker service, or better results, they probably will not care. If you haven't got a good answer to that, then you need to put your thinking cap on and figure it out. If you can't put into words how you are different from every other law firm in town and why your customers should care, then they probably will not care, and you probably are not different from your competition at all. Be honest with yourself, and don't try to fabricate something out of nothing.

Brand

What's your brand? We used to think of *brand* as a logo or group of stylized words and colors. Clever marketers even dream up fanciful words like *ultra-surfactant quotient* and *X-43 Super Clean* to push their brands. Since the beginning of time, clever marketers have been trying to come up with more and more fantastic adjectives to describe their products to make them seem more interesting: "Buy Thor's wheels, cut round for a smoother ride!" Savvy consumers and businesses don't fall for code words or slick logos as a replacement for the values of the company.

Your brand should be an extension of what your firm is, what it stands for, and how it does business. If that sounds like a tall order, it is. Creating the perfect marketing package takes more than just combining your services with cool logos to create a brand. And branding is far more than just fancy marketing. While the slick marketing piece will help play a role, it's the marriage of your brand message with the actions of the firm that ultimately matter. In other words, reality must match your branding, or your customers will consider it all just more hype.

You have to first understand that all businesses are really providing a service. And what's worse, today's on-line virtual world has turned every competitor in the world into *your* competitor. The only real distinction comes down to service. It's not what you sell. It's how you sell it. It's not what you promise in brochures and advertising campaigns. It's how you support your customers during the process and after the service is provided or the case is won. How does your brand tell that story and does the brand story match the reality?

Mission/Vision Statement

A mission statement is a simple statement of what business you are in and why. This statement is the responsibility of the owners and senior management of a company to define and implement. Once written, the mission statement serves as the ground rules for operating the business. That is, each major decision of the firm should somehow support the mission or vision of the organization. Small business owners ask whether the mission statement isn't just some big company nonsense made up by Fortune 500 executives without a real job. We think the mission statement is just as important for small companies, maybe more important, than for their multinational counterparts. You should be able to use your mission statement to guide the firm as you grow. If you are considering new ventures or service lines, they should first be measured against your mission statement and whether they support the overall goals of the organization. If not, you should reconsider the venture or your mission. All activities of your company should further your mission.

Without a clearly defined statement that you support and believe, you may wander aimlessly among your competitors, trying different courses and taking different paths without any real goal. Especially for a small firm, your mission statement should be a defining document of your beliefs and objectives for going into the practice of law in the first place.

A mission statement can be a simple sentence, a declaration, or a more complete summary of an organization's beliefs, values, and vision for its future. If you have a strong drive and vision for your firm, here is your chance to share that belief and value system with your employees and customers.

For a mission or value statement to be effective in guiding your firm's direction and operations, it should be a clearly stated and honestly held declaration of your beliefs, not some phony corporate speak. Your mission is a basic statement describing the overall purpose of your firm. It is the first strategic decision the firm should take. The mission should define your direction, priorities, and what sets you apart from your competitors. It should reflect the personality of the owners and help build the image of the organization. Ideally, it will motivate your staff and clarify the direction you will take on your path to success.

Whether your mission statement is long and involved or short and sweet, it must be real. Your customers and employees will be turned off by marketing hype that doesn't reflect the way you behave. Keep in mind that your clients are not attorneys. If your mission, slogan, or values statement sounds as if it came out of a LexisNexis™ search, they will not be impressed. The mission statement should not only speak to you and your staff but also be something that your customers can read and embrace.

Generally speaking, the competition bar is set extremely low. Many larger firms develop slogans and mission statements to promote their brand and end up shooting themselves in the foot. You're not writing for your law professor; you're writing for your employees and your customers. If your customers are law professors, then fine. But I'm guessing you have a different clientele.

It's hard to find good examples of mission statements from actual law firms since few of them are bold enough to publish a mission statement and those that do rarely get it right. Here's an example of what we consider a good mission statement morphed from a couple of real firms to protect the guilty.

We believe in building a firm of attorneys and support staff who exemplify the virtues of integrity, honesty, reliability, and resourcefulness.

We believe that every person and every business, from a single employee to a large corporation, deserves the right to legal counsel without having to suffer financially.

We believe that our client's time is more valuable than our own – and we pledge to behave in a way that supports that belief.

Service

What are your services? You should be able to define your services or practice lines in terms of what it does for the customer. How does it make the customer's life better, easier, faster, or cheaper? How will your customer's life be improved by buying your service? What makes your services superior to every other similar legal service already on the market?

Describe, in detail, the services you will be selling. Your description should include a general description of each service, plus pricing models and distribution channels for each.

Your firm's strengths and weaknesses will help you evaluate which opportunities are right for you and the threats to avoid. As you develop your service offerings, keep in mind the needs, wants, and desires of your target customer. You might think that the latest add-on or upgrade is the hottest next thing in the market, but does your customer? Many people have designed and marketed them only to find that no real market exists. If a company spent lots of money developing marketing plans and buying advertising and if there was no real market for a service, then the funds were wasted.

Talk to your customers, conduct focus groups, or perform other market studies. Make sure that your prospective customers actually want to pay money for your particular service. One way is to select some individuals who are in your target customer group and ask them. If the difference in quantity, flavor, hourly rate, and delivery method is potentially important to the marketing effort, take the necessary time to understand these factors. If your plan is big and the risk is high, you might need to hire a market research firm to help determine which characteristics should be included in your services.

Features versus Benefits

Make sure you understand the difference between features and benefits. A feature is a factual statement about a service; it's what a service offers. A benefit is what those features mean; it describes why your customer should care. Theodore Levitt, a 19th-century economist and Harvard University professor, described the difference like this: "People don't want to buy a quarter-inch drill; they want a quarter-inch hole."

Think about a business that sells products. The customers care only about benefits. They are what's in it for me kind of people. In fact, everyone is a what's in it for me kind of person. The producer cares about product features: it has a little handle here, this one is blue, that button makes it fly higher, and those straps are double secured. As consumers, the customers care only about the product benefits: it's easy to carry, it matches their carpets, they can feel the exhilaration, and it's safe. Just keep in mind that you care only about features. Your clients care only about benefits.

So let's apply this thinking to a legal environment. In the following table, the left column lists features that you care about, and the right column lists benefits that your clients care about.

FEATURES	BENEFITS
Harvard Law Degree	Prepare briefs quicker, saving you money
15 Years Experience	Prepare better defense by knowing tendencies of local judges
Large Firm	One stop shopping for legal needs
Small Firm	Personalized service designed for your business needs
Small Business Focus	We'll help manage your litigation expense so you'll be more profitable
Contracts Specialty	We'll develop contracts to manage your specific risks to save you money

Properly selling your firm means selling your benefits, not pushing features. Benefits are what matter to your clients, so make sure they understand how doing business with you will make their life better or business more profitable.

Pricing

What will you charge for your services? Why? Will you have different pricing models for individual clients versus business clients? How do your rates compare to those of your competitors? How do your rates compare to your overhead? What are the benefits of being cheaper than your competitors? Are there benefits to being more expensive? How will you use payment terms and customer accounts to support your sales and financial goals?

Distribution Channels

We discussed distribution channels at length during the research section. You should understand how your industry and target market segment(s) operate. How will you get your services to your customers? Will you utilize your own staff and attorneys to sell? Analyze your choices, and make a decision that best serves you and your customers.

Promotion Goals

Marketing plans don't have to be complicated, but they do need to be well thought out. Identifying where you want to be or what outcome you hope to see from your efforts will help you lay out specific action plans to achieve the success you desire.

Identify the Goals

What do you want the marketing plan to accomplish? How long will it take? You need to establish specific market objectives and time frames for accomplishing your goals. If you haven't identified specifics, at best you'll spin your wheels and not accomplish much. At worst, you'll throw away a pile of money and get nothing out of it.

Identify the Message

What's the message you want your customers to associate with your firm name or services? Keep it simple, descriptive of some benefit to your customers or problem solved, and differentiate your firm from your competitors. Do you have a secret weapon? Do you have a specialty that nobody else has? If you do, great; use it to your advantage. If not, you need to keep your message focused on your customers, fulfilling their needs and solving their problems.

Identify the Budget

How much will you spend? Don't start asking that question when you get the bill from the advertising sales rep. Define the budget for marketing your service upfront when developing the plan, and then manage it.

How Will You Measure?

How will you measure and how will you define success? It's important to identify these issues before you begin. If you don't know what the end result should look like, how will you know if you got there or not? And if you don't get what you hoped for, how will you change your plan to better achieve your goals?

You will need a way to test your results so that you can make improvements to the plan. If you're looking at a radio spot to promote a particular service, maybe you run two different spots to determine which wording and portrayal work best. Maybe two different print ads could be used to see which draws more calls from interested customers. Make sure to include a different website, phone number, e-mail, or identifier so that you can tell which ad drove which result. Some people will remember a radio spot from several years ago or confuse a competitor's ad with one from your business.

You must constantly monitor, measure, and test your promotional programs for effectiveness. If they aren't working, figure out why, and make the necessary changes. Don't launch a promotional campaign, and then forget about it. The ad sales people love customers who do that. They can sell you spots without ever having to answer for the promotional effectiveness. That's the same as a big tattoo on your forehead that says, "Sucker!"

Promotion Tactics

Before we start developing an action plan for promoting your firm, let's look at some of the common tactics used in business generally. Think of this as more of a general definitions chapter of some of the major tactic possibilities. In the next section, we'll take these general tactical ideas and turn them into a plan specifically for attorneys.

Promotion Tactics

Advertising and Promotion
Public Relations
Networking
Action Plan

This is an opportunity for you to be creative. There are as many tactics for promoting your business as there are people who can think of creative ways of promoting. From setting up a company Facebook page to advertising on cardboard tavern coasters, the whole world is open for your use. The key is getting your brand specific message to your target clientele. As long you keep that key principal in mind, the more creative your tactic, the better.

Advertising and Promotion

Typically, the difference between "advertising" and "promotion" is money. You have to pay for advertising whereas promotion is free. The lines are fairly blurry when discussing some forms of advertising, so let's lump them together and call it all advertising. For a small business, you're always going to try to get the most bang for your buck. If you can get something for free or nearly free, then you'll do it. We don't think it's all that important to draw a distinction between paid advertising and free promotion. Let's just agree to call it all advertising and realize that some you'll have to pay for and some you won't.

Advertising for your small firm can take many different forms, from television or radio spots to sponsoring the high school yearbook. Advertising can easily become a black hole where money goes and never returns. This is one area in which having a well-defined budget and expectations is important. Know upfront how much you can spend in advertising and how you will measure your success. If your first attempt doesn't work, change your approach or change your form. Many advertising options for small business fall under the category of "donations" rather than advertising. Don't expect a high school yearbook ad to double your new sales leads. However, advertising in a sports or arts program may lead to new customers. Which form of advertising you use will depend on your customer base and service line. If you're new at this, it's usually a good idea to take small steps so that you can measure your success before spending big bucks on a full-blown campaign.

The whole idea in advertising is to get your message to your customers. You don't care to get your message to people or businesses that aren't target customers. Spending money to spread your message in the wrong place or to the wrong people is just wasting money.

Let's take a look at some examples of advertising.

Websites

Every business needs a website, period. If you have no intentions of using your site for the recruitment of customers, then you need it for general reference. In today's business environment, a business without a website is not viewed as a serious business. Even if your site is only serving as a business card with contact information and hours of operation, it's often the first impression you give to potential customers. Websites are easy to create and cheap. There's really no excuse for not having some kind of web presence.

When we consider doing business with a new company, the first thing we do is look at their website. If they don't have one, or it's really crummy, we try to find an alternative company with which to do business. And while that sentiment is not true for every consumer, you really can't afford to turn away any likely consumers.

Marketing Collateral

From business cards to brochures and from product data sheets to samples, marketing collateral should define your brand and your services. Most small business owners can't afford fancy Madison Avenue created marketing material. Consider how you can stretch your budget to get the best material available. Even if you don't have much of a budget, don't put out crummy material. Some items can be printed or even copied in black and white on a copier. For the typical small business owner, a product data sheet or Material Safety Data Sheet (MSDS) probably doesn't need to be a four-color print job. If you have to choose between good design and good color/materials/printing, choose good design. A well designed marketing piece can be used for many years. As your budget increases, you can change the printing or medium to spruce up the piece. However, a cheap design will look cheap no matter how fancy the printing or paper.

If you can only afford to produce one good piece of marketing collateral, make it your business card. You'll hand out your business card several hundred times a year. In many cases, your business card will be the only piece of collateral that a prospective customer will see. Spend the extra money to get your card designed by a professional so that you can always put your best foot forward with every contact.

Direct Marketing

Direct marketing can include such approaches as direct mail, e-mail, phone solicitation, and lead generation. If you are using purchased mailing or calling lists, it's important to first define the type of lead for which you are looking. Most list agencies will be able to sort out their database into subgroups that meet your criteria. For example, if a business is selling industrial supplies and equipment, it doesn't do any good to solicit families. If a business is selling cosmetics, they are probably wasting their time soliciting sporting venues. The more clearly you can define your customers, the better your list agency will be able to define the list you purchase.

Depending on your practice and market, direct mail may be an excellent choice for contacting customers and generating leads. This is where getting a good list is really important. Define your customers, and purchase a list that is as close to it as possible.

Social Media

Social media has become a popular promotional tactic in the past couple of years. It's based on the premise that by building personal relationships with people, they will be more likely to buy your services when they need them or recommend your firm to a friend who is in need of your specialties. It can be a bit of a challenge to justify this activity in terms of time and costs because it seems to be a large black hole where you pour your time. However, the costs associated with social networking activities are low in terms of hard dollars spent. It's really a question of your time.

There are dozens of different social networking sites, and different brands pop up every day. As of the writing of this book, the following social networking sites were fairly effective for mainstream work.

Twitter: This micro blogging site enables users to send "tweets," messages of 140 characters or less. It's an excellent tool for communicating with clients and presenting your brand. The search engines apparently give tweets favorable recognition, and heavy keyword use can bring traffic to your site.

Facebook: This is a social networking site where users can add information, communicate with friends, send messages, and build an elaborate profile complete with pictures, video, and games. Facebook has recently added the ability to create business pages, an area that is growing rapidly. The complete extent of the benefit is yet unknown, as this medium is in the infancy stage. I expect it will continue to grow and become one of the most favored venues for businesses, even more important than a company web page in the future. Facebook is excellent for engaging people who like your firm or for promoting your brand.

LinkedIn: This is a social networking site for business professionals. It's essentially an elaborate professional resume. The service is an excellent means of branding for a professional, but it does less than most other sites at communicating to a particular group and generating traffic.

YouTube: This is a video sharing website where users can upload and share videos. YouTube has seen phenomenal growth in recent years and is one of the best social networking sites for corporate branding, communication with customers, and promotion of your website.

Please recognize that by the time I finish typing this page, the social media players will have changed. These are just a few of the more important players in the social media market as of early 2012. There are fast moving media, and they require a considerable time investment. However, the payoff is huge traffic, brand awareness, and customer communication.

Newspaper

Most newspapers have several opportunities for paid advertising and free promotion in the course of a weekly news cycle. Paid advertising is the most obvious method. As with any paid advertising, you want to make sure the paper's readership demographics matches your target customers. Many newspapers today have a print version of the paper and an on-line version. Check the demographics of each, and determine whether either version is a good match to your target customer demographics.

In addition to buying an actual ad, you can also use some of the free or nearly free options available in the paper. Most papers have a section that runs weekly in the Sunday paper that lists newsmakers in business. This is an opportunity to highlight new employees, promotions of existing employees, or awards to or significant accomplishments by you or your employees. The calendar of events is an opportunity for you to list open houses and speaking events that you or your employees are leading.

Industry Advertising

Most industries have professional journals and magazines that cover the news and newsmakers in that industry. This can be a good venue for advertising, if the demographic fits your needs. The benefit of industry publications is that the target audience tends to be focused in a particular area.

Radio and TV Advertising

Radio and TV advertising can be very effective for your business, if the venue and time slot deliver the appropriate demographics. Attorneys have to be very careful that their target clientele is actually represented in a station's demographics. Frank discussions with the advertising rep for each station about your intentions and targets will be helpful. If the rep can't deliver the demographic you need, go elsewhere. Don't get suckered into trying a program if the audience isn't right.

Outdoor Advertising

From interstate logos to electronic billboards, outdoor advertising has the ability to put your business in front of drivers. Outdoor advertising has the flexibility to change the message frequently while keeping your branding consistent. Whether you're looking to "skin" a personal vehicle or truck with your firm's logo or your headshot, adorn a park bench with a message about your intellectual property services, or just notify local drivers to get their will updated, outdoor signage becomes a popular advertising medium. The low cost and flexibility make it ideal for many business ventures.

Public Relations

While public relations has a different meaning in a large corporate setting, small business can use many free methods to get their word out. It is in this context that I refer to public relations for small business. Some examples are:

Press Releases

One of best tools in the small business owner's public relations toolbox is the press release. A well written press release is bound to get some mention in the local business section of the newspaper. In the best possible scenario, this might lead to an article or television interview. News outlets are constantly looking for interesting news and public interest stories. While they have lots of national and state stories they can carry, they'd much rather tell a local story. You just need to give them a compelling reason to do so.

When writing a press release, follow the standard industry format. If you don't know how to write a press release, then do a little research so that you can utilize the proper format and tell a newsworthy story. If your press release is seen as an advertisement, it likely won't get mentioned. The local media want to help; you just have to do your part.

By becoming an industry resource to the business editor or one of the reporters that covers your profession, you stand a greater chance of getting your news release turned into a story in the paper or on the TV news. When you see interesting or important news articles or professional papers about your markets, share that information with the reporter or editor. By being helpful and not self-serving with your information, you're more likely to be seen as a credible news source when it comes time to get your story covered.

Once you've written your press release, you can e-mail it to the editors of the appropriate industry journals and magazines, as well as section editors of newspapers. Just copy the press release into the e-mail body. Don't send it as an attachment, as it might not get opened. Newspapers typically have low budgets, and many can't open the latest version of MS Office formatted products. In some cases, we've had editors tell us they can't open a PDF formatted document. In addition, post the press release on your website for all visitors to see, including search engine spiders. Posting it on your site will give you the net permanence that you need for search engine listings.

If you want wider distribution, you can use free and paid press release services. Free services will have a more limited distribution, and many times will lack permanence on the web, but they are free. Do a little research to determine which of the many free sites to use. Not all free press release sites are appropriate for all industries.

Paid press release services will get you wide distribution, including international sites. Your press release will have a permanent net presence available for search engines to find and rank and usually will come with some level of customer service. These services will allow you to select markets, outlets, and industries. These services typically charge $250 to $750 per release.

Blogs

A blog is a means to converse with your customers and followers and share information in a casual and direct manner. Link the blog to your website. Anyone can write and manage a blog. It's not about writing a novel. In fact, short, to the point stories are the norm. If you're going to write consistently long articles, then they must be entertaining and/or informative. People aren't going to read a three-page article that drones on about nothing.

Your blog entries can be a combination of information about your practice, your profession, special events at your firm, interesting stories about your employees, and even special rates. It can't be a constant sales pitch, however. If it is, no one will come back.

Charity and Civic Volunteer

Become a volunteer with a local charity or civic group. Pick a group that you have interest in and get to work. A leadership role with a well-known or respected civic or charitable group will give you, your employees, and your firm credibility, not to mention notice of the good work that the group is doing in your community. I've never seen a company that adopted a "give back" attitude get anything but a positive response from their good work in the community.

If you have expertise in particular areas of your profession, offer to teach classes in those areas to local entrepreneurs. Local business incubators and small business development centers are always looking for volunteers to help inform the public, mentor entrepreneurs, and lead training classes. This can be a good way of gaining credibility within the business community and among the public. By associating yourself with worthwhile organizations that help others learn what you've already learned, you are seen as an expert in your field.

Speaker and Workshop Leader

In addition to speaking and mentoring in certain settings, you can offer classes on your own and give talks. Find a local restaurant, hotel, or business services company to donate space in return for bringing in customers. You can give a free or paid talk or conduct a workshop on a topic that your customer base will hopefully find interesting. By giving the talk or conducting the workshop, you gain credibility as an expert in your field.

Most civic groups that meet regularly, such as the Rotary Club, need speakers to entertain and inform their membership. Depending on the size of your community, there will be from three to dozens of these type groups that are regularly seeking speakers.

Networking

Networking is a free or low-cost promotion strategy that puts you in front of customers, competitors, other local business owners, employees, and individuals who can help promote your firm by word of mouth. While there are many organized networking events through business groups or civic clubs, it can also take place in a casual and opportunistic way.

If you are a member of local business groups, such as the chamber of commerce or a BNI group, don't attempt to meet as many people as possible and hand out all your business cards. The idea with networking is to make deep connections with a few selected individuals and bring value to the relationship. That is, find out about the other individuals' businesses and find ways to make connections, introductions, or referrals for them.

Don't try to make a sale in the first five minutes of talking. In fact, don't try to make a sale at all. Successful networking is about giving, not getting. If you give on your side of the relationship, the other side will do the same. You will build valuable business relationships and over time have a network of people promoting your firm for you.

Networking is a long-term process. It will not always generate immediate results. While you may get lucky, plan on developing a network of business partners and friends who support one another, direct leads to one another, and serve as resources to support one another's businesses. We'll discuss a specific plan for networking in the next chapter.

The Elevator Pitch

"So, what do you do?" How do you answer this question? It's called the elevator pitch, and it may be the most important 30 seconds of your business life. Whether at a cocktail party, convention, business meeting, or chance meeting, you are frequently asked what you do and have only a short window to engage your target with a compelling and interesting response that will make him or her ask more questions about your business.

An elevator pitch is a *brief* statement about who you are, what your business does, and why anyone should care. The emphasis should be on why anyone should care. Here's the idea: you're in an elevator with a potential business investor or customer, and he or she asks what you do. You have about 30 seconds, or the length of the elevator ride, to tell the individual about your business and get him or her intrigued enough to keep talking to you when you reach the lobby. In most cases, if you haven't said something interesting in the first 10 seconds, the listener will probably quit listening and look for an opportunity to leave your presence.

Write out your elevator pitch and practice saying it in a relaxed and confident tone. You will need different elevator pitches for different situations and audiences. The only way to get good at this is to script the pitch and practice delivering it. Often you'll find that in saying out loud what you have written, it doesn't really work. Don't just read your script in your mind; say it out loud, and practice in front of people who can give you constructive criticism.

What should you include in your elevator pitch? Here are a few thoughts to help you craft your ideal message:

How are you unique? Why are your firm's services any different from those of your competitors?

Speak to your customer's pain: Nobody cares that you have a special certification and continuing education credits in the IRS code. But if you have a strategy to help save companies reduce their tax liability by restructuring their real estate portfolio, now that might be really helpful and interesting to certain clients.

Make it interesting: An excellent elevator pitch should get you pumped up. If you're flat and lifeless, why would your prospect care what you're saying? If you have a great story or passion, work that into your pitch.

Keep it simple: You can't make a single story work for every situation and every prospect. You need to build an arsenal of components that you know backwards and forwards that can be woven together for just the right message for each audience. Write down each message variation and rewrite them until they are perfect. This is the time to pick just the right wording and color for your pitch. Then practice, practice, practice.

It's not about you: In case you missed that point already, it's about your clientele and how you can make their life better. Your customers do not care about you; they care only about themselves. If you can keep that point in mind, you'll have a better chance of developing an interesting elevator pitch.

Action Plan

The action plan phase of the marketing plan is really a two-step process. First, you identify the specific tactic you'll use, and then you create the action plan to make it happen. Putting these various tactics into practice is the key to the marketing plan. If you don't actually do something, nothing will happen, and all that time spent researching and planning will be wasted. Develop a system for managing your marketing tactics that works for you and your firm, or use the simple system that we've developed for small business owners to manage the process.

We like to use a simple spreadsheet to identify the various tactics that a business is using—when the particular tactic takes place during the year, who is responsible, and what's the budget. This gives you an overall look at your particular tactics and when they are slated to run. You can define the time frame as cells in the spreadsheet that correspond to a month or week within the year. Assign a color to the cell when the tactic is supposed to run. You can assign meanings to different colors that represent when deadlines occur for a particular event, such as a magazine ad or a special promotion effort in the newspaper or on the radio. The spreadsheet is your visualization of the entire process.

On a separate spreadsheet, identify each tactic, and list the individual actions that are required for successful implementation. Again, use the individual spreadsheet cells to identify time frames. You are essentially creating a little Gantt chart of the individual activities involved in the tactic. Let's look at two example tactics and some of the individual activities that might be involved.

Example Tactic 1: Cable TV advertisement during the daytime aimed at senior citizens.

Our example company is a local law firm that specializes in elder law that will promote estate planning services to seniors with an advertising campaign on cable TV.

Individual activities required: The firm will identify the specific activities involved in the successful completion of this tactic; the employees involved and responsible for each activity; and the budget associated with each. They will confirm the critical path(s), and back-date each activity so that it can be started in time to meet the individual deadlines.

Identify the specific goal of the advertisement: The firm wants to promote elder law services, such as estate planning and wills. The firm made a strategic decision to move into this area and has hired two experienced attorneys to oversee this practice area. In previous years, only 5% of the firm's business was in this area. By year-end, the firm hopes to increase elder law services to 15% and 25% by end of the second year.

Identify TV deadlines: The firm will discuss time deadlines for writing, shooting, and editing the video with the cable sales representative. The firm wants the ads running at least two weeks prior to an AARP convention in town in three months. All other activities related to producing the video will be scheduled based on that deadline. All physical activities relating to the new business increase in the firm will be back-dated based on the first run date of the ad. These two dates are what's known as the critical path. All activities related to each of these dates will be scheduled based on having the action completed before the deadline.

Create a special service offering: The two new attorneys will develop a special service offering, especially for the TV spot sales. They will work with the accounting manager to ensure that the pricing makes sense for the firm and is affordable for the target audience.

Create the ad: The firm will work with the outside marketing group to create the story, identify the target audience, and set the broad goals. The marketing group will create the script and flow of the commercial, and then select appropriate actors. After approving the story board and actor selection, the firm will give the marketing group the approval to shoot the spot. After shooting, the marketing group will complete editing and prepare a preview for the firm's partner approval.

Confirm labor requirements: An increase of 15% in elder law services will require two new administrative/legal assistants and one new associate. The firm will hire the assistants one month in advance of the run date of the spot to allow for appropriate training. The new associate will be hired one week in advance of the spot and will begin working with the lead attorney to get on-the-job training.

Hire additional employees: New labor requirements will be given to the human resource department or outside staffing company to bring in new employees in time to get them trained for the new business activity.

Train employees: The new assistants will be trained with in-house resources, as well as outside workshops and seminars so that they are prepared for the volume of new business generated by the TV spots.

Example Tactic 2: Create a Twitter account for an attorney providing business start-up services.

Our example company is a local lawyer who specializes in business start-up services, such as forming business entities, partnership agreements, and contracts.

Individual activities required: The attorney will identify the specific activities involved in the successful completion of this tactic; the employees responsible for each activity; and the budget associated with each. They will confirm the critical path(s), and back-date each activity so that it can be started in time to meet the individual deadlines.

Identify the specific goal of the activity: The attorney wants to promote business start-up services and increase awareness of the firm and reputation in the region. The main goal of the activity is to increase firm credibility in the business community. A recent survey by the attorney showed only average results in awareness and credibility of the firm among the business community. The attorney is hoping for a steady increase in survey results from what will be a yearly survey measurement. There is no specific business increase in terms of dollars or percentages but rather an increase in awareness and credibility.

Identify requirements: The attorney will discuss the realities of running a Twitter account with the firm's administrative assistant who is knowledgeable in social media. This person will identify the frequency of posts, the percentages of post types that best support the tactic goals, and the available tools to assist with the job of physically scheduling the posts. In addition, the attorney and assistant will discuss their respective roles in responding to mentions and questions, following others, and engaging in conversations with other account holders.

Create a posting schedule: The assistant will create and schedule the regular posts based on their goals. The attorney will devote certain time slots in the day to respond to others on the Twitter platform.

In order for a tactic to be successful, it should have a goal, a specific activity plan, and a means for measuring whether the tactic was successful. Just deciding to engage in an activity and handing it off to an assistant is not going to turn into success. While you can and should use the most cost- and time-efficient employee for the job, you must identify the goals and help outline the plan before handing it off. In the case of social media, you will have to have an active voice in the tactic in order for it to be well received and considered authentic.

The Attorney Action Plan

The action plan phase of your marketing plan could have dozens of different tactics for promoting and advertising your services or firm. The specific tactics you choose will depend on your individual situation, budget, goals, and time frame. We'll cover some of the more common ways to promote your services and divide the list into Phase 1, Phase 2, and Phase 3 items. The Phase 1 items are the tactics that we recommend for all law firms. Frankly, you should already be doing these. These are the basic promotional tactics that, if done properly and consistently, will increase your business. The Phase 2 items should be the list that you're starting to work on to improve your marketing. Hopefully, you are already doing some of these or have done some of these in the past. If so, these items will begin to place you in searches. The Phase 3 items may be new to you or may have been what you expected to see when you bought this book. These are the organized advertising tactics.

Phase 1 Tactics
Brand Refresher
Elevator Pitch
Business Cards
Website
Networking

Phase 2 Tactics
Blogs and Article Writing
Social Media
Workshops
Public Speaking
Videos

Phase 3 Tactics
Print
Internet
Radio/TV
Guerilla Tactics

Attorney Treasure Chest

The possible tactics are only limited by your imagination and creativity. However, the specific tactics you select will be based on your brand and your customer base. Just because we listed items as possibilities doesn't mean you have to do each one.

As you design your particular action plan, keep in mind your professional ethics, your mission, and/or vision statement. This part should keep you out of trouble with the ethics police. Then start thinking of ways to get your brand message in front of your customers. In fact, everything you do from a promotion standpoint should start with your brand. You must develop your brand and then build the tactics to support the brand. If you don't start with the brand, your message will be muddled and inconsistent—a recipe for being ignored.

Phase 1 Tactics

Phase 1 Tactics are the high priority tactics. These are the tactics every law firm should already be doing. If not, implement them as soon as possible. Phase 1 tactics are the one exception to the "you don't have to do everything on the list" caution. You should implement all Phase 1 tactics.

Brand Refresher

We realize that if you follow the process outlined in this book, you will have already revamped or created in the first place a brand that identifies your business and reflects on your style, values, and customer base. But we also realize that many of you who are already in business just skipped that part, thinking that you already have nice branding. If you followed the outline and have already worked on this step, you can move on. If you skipped that part earlier, take a look at your brand from the perspective of your clientele and your mission or values statement. Do these pieces work well together or does your branding need an update? If you are not happy or you think your brand might not be putting your firm's best foot forward, then get some help. There are decent to exceptional branding companies all over the country.

Here's the deal: you are an attorney. You know the law. You have studied the law and one or more practical areas of the world for six or eight or maybe even 10 years. We're guessing, however, that you never studied marketing and branding. This isn't the time to decide you know everything and try it yourself. If you have only a small budget for the first year, spend some of it here. Spend the *first* money on your brand. If you only have enough money to do a little, then get your brand updated and get some great business cards. Your brand is the foundation of your marketing plan, and your business card is the cornerstone.

Elevator Pitch

"So, what do you do?" When you're asked that question, will you be able to respond appropriately? We covered this in the previous section, so just make sure you have different versions of your elevator pitch ready when the moment arises. Practice these different varieties of your elevator pitch out loud to your partners or spouse. The first time your elevator pitch comes out of your mouth shouldn't be to a potential client.

Business Cards

For many of you, your business card will be the first piece and in some cases, the only piece of marketing material that your potential client will see. Yes, we know you can get $20 business cards at several sites on the Internet. Don't do it! Do you want to make a great first impression on every potential client you meet or save $100 to $150 on business cards?

Your marketing/branding company partner will help you design an appropriate business card that not only supports your brand but also sets you apart from your competition. If you can afford only to do one thing, get a great business card. If you don't know how to make a great impression with your business card, get some professional help. You really should not skimp here.

You will be handing out your card on a regular basis all year long. Make sure that you are handing out a piece of marketing collateral that makes a good first impression, sets you apart from every other attorney in town, and creates a call to action. If you have to explain what you do to people who see your card, it's not going to be very effective. Through words, images, and colors, your business card should be able to sell your firm by itself. It should serve as a reminder to your clients or potential clients to call you for advice or service.

Create business cards for every employee in your firm, from the founding partner to the newest administrative assistant. Every single employee in your firm should be selling your services with a business card. Lower level employees will gladly hand out business cards to their friends and relatives, especially if you encourage them to spread them around. Don't miss a great opportunity to let your clerk, administrative assistant, legal assistant, or paralegal sell your firm.

Now that you have a great business card, how can you use it to improve your marketing? Here's a small list of creative possibilities. Some or none of these tactics might be right for you. You have to make that determination based on your brand, your customers, and your goals.

- Add a coupon.
- Lead people to your website for information, discounts, free stuff, or advice.
- Add a conversion chart (interest rates, restaurant tipping, and calendar).
- Create a "notes" area on the back.
- Insert your cards in appropriate books at the local library.
- Handwrite a note on the back of your card, and include it with correspondence or invoices.

Website

Let's start here: every business should have a website, period. Especially if you are in the service business, you need a way to tell your story. And don't have a "website under construction" sign; have an actual website. If you spent all your marketing dollars on business cards and now have nothing left for a website, then do it yourself. Use a free blog site to create a website. You must have something. A potential customer looking you up on the Internet that sees "under construction" or nothing will likely pass you by as not a real firm or conclude (probably rightly) that you just aren't that professional. Even if you can't have a killer website, you must at least have some sort of website. Seriously, having nothing is just not an option for an attorney.

Your website tells a lot about your business. Look around at other attorney websites from your community or any community. You're going to see dull, very professional fonts and subdued color schemes that just scream, "Don't look at me; I'm incredibly uninteresting!" If your firm's website looks like this, maybe it's time to rethink your website.

If you are starting from scratch or rethinking your website, begin by thinking about the purpose of your site. What do you hope to accomplish by sending prospects there? Some examples are:

- Educate and inform potential customers.
- Sell services.
- Extend the current advertising plan.
- Explain a sales offer.
- Provide better customer service.
- Develop prospects.
- Strengthen brand identity.

Getting started with a website isn't as hard as you might think. Follow these steps to get a basic website that will serve you well.

Website Step 1: Purpose

Think about the purpose(s) of your website before you start the design process. Make sure that the design, navigation, copy, and images support that purpose. Again, this is an area where a professional would be a big plus if you have the budget.

Website Step 2: Keywords

Find the keywords for your niche. Use Google AdWords or another keyword tool to find the search terms that people are using to get information or find websites in your practice area(s). If you create a website that no one finds, is it really there? Make a list of the appropriate keywords for your niche or practice areas, and keep them handy. You will use this list of words as you create your site and copy.

Website Step 3: Domain Name

This may be the hardest step of all. Select an appropriate domain name that is actually available. The domain name is your website address (www.examplename.com). You want a keyword rich domain that is appropriate for your firm. This is difficult because all of the most interesting names have already been taken. We recommend selecting a name that is easy to remember, is short, is as similar to your firm name as possible, and most importantly is a .com address. Don't be tempted to use a .biz, .org, .net, or .us address as your primary address. Feel free to grab those varieties and common misspellings of your firm name and have them point to your main site, but don't use them as your primary address except as a last resort.

There are many different domain registrars to select from. You can use a firm that only handles the domain registration or one that also hosts websites and other services. You should be able to register a domain for less than $20 a year.

Website Step 4: Create Layout and Navigation

Before you start writing copy and inserting pictures, think about the overall look and feel of the site. How will the pages be laid out, where will the navigation be located, how many pages you will use, whether you'll use subpages, and so forth? Sketch out the layout of your pages on a piece of paper, and lay the pages side by side so you can see the whole site in front of you. Again, if you need professional help, get it.

Think about the logical flow from page to page to make sure you have a consistency in how your information flows. Your navigation should be laid out in the logical categories that your clients will understand. If you aren't sure, have your friends or kids look at the navigation and get their response. The more information that is available within one or two clicks, the better. Don't bury your content five to eight clicks deep if you want anyone to actually find it.

If you are using a template site, select an interesting template, and the navigation will come with it. You probably won't have to worry about the navigation, as the site will automatically name the navigation links based on your page name.

Website Step 5: Create Content

Create content that utilizes the keywords you researched earlier. Think about short paragraphs, lists, and bullets. Don't create massive paragraphs full of description because people will not read it. Write your content as a newspaper writer would. Use paragraphs with two to four short sentences. Get to the point quickly, and give just enough additional information as you need to describe your services. We've become very lazy consumers, so keep that in mind as you create your descriptions and tell your story.

With your keywords in mind, write your copy so that it tells your story in a way that is interesting to your customer. You are creating this website for your customers, not yourself. Don't use overly technical jargon that isn't understood by your customer base. If you can't find the words or don't have the time to be creative yourself, hire a local writer to create the content for you. There are lots of underemployed writers just looking for interesting work. There are also websites where you can hire people to do all sorts of technical and administrative tasks for a small fee. We have used www.elance.com in the past with good success. There are other sites that function similarly.

Use interesting graphics that are appropriate for your content. People love pictures. You should use your own graphics and pictures whenever possible. If you need to buy pictures, get them from a royalty-free distributor. There are many good websites that offer pictures for use in articles, blogs, websites, and so forth that are inexpensive and don't require a royalty payment for every view. You will pay a small one-time fee for the use of the picture. You can get high quality photographs in a variety of subjects. If you search the Internet for "royalty-free photographs," you'll find several websites that offer this service. You shouldn't have to pay more than $3 to $7 for these pictures.

Website Step 6: Use Video

To help tell your story, use video. Most sites will allow you to upload video content to YouTube or other video hosting sites and link it to your firm's site. This gives you the double advantage of having additional content on YouTube where potential customers can see it. People love video because it tells a story quickly and shows the personality of the speaker. You can get a lot of information out quickly in video form. You can tell a story in a minute or two that otherwise would take pages of copy to convey. People will gladly listen to a 30-second to three-minute video whereas they would never read three pages of copy. Limit your video's length to three minutes. Unless you have a complicated topic or are educating your clients, they probably will not watch a long video.

A mini workshop type video with which you convey information about a complicated topic that is of interest to your customers could be 10 to 30 minutes in length. On the one hand, recognize that only a small percentage of customers will actually watch a video piece like that. On the other hand, a video like this may generate leads to your site from outside of your regular customer base. Go back to the notion of lazy consumers; people would much rather watch a 10- to 30-minute video than read a lengthy white paper.

You can use video to tell a story about how your firm was started, how you got interested in the law, how to select an attorney that's right for the client, how to create a will, or most any topic that makes sense for your practice. Video is one of the best tools available for helping your site place high in Internet searches, and isn't that why we're doing this in the first place? So people will find your site and do something?

Website Step 7: Attorney Bio

Make sure to create a complete bio for each attorney. Many potential clients will go here first to see your picture and learn about your background, qualifications, and interests. Be sure to list community and civic activities in which you are involved. Don't skimp on the information you include. Include a professional headshot at a minimum. If you can afford it, include a video introduction.

The type of information you include here is really dependent on your brand. If you are selling your firm as a top shelf corporate firm, you're going to want to craft your partner and associate bios so that they reflect that sort of professionalism. Focusing on education, training, and capabilities should be your priority. If you are positioning yourself as a friendly elder law practice, much more personal information about your attorneys and staff is appropriate. In either case, a little personal information about your attorneys is good. Even with a corporate firm, your clients are still people, and people want to do business with people they like and trust. At a minimum, get enough personal information out to enable people to make a connection with your partners, associates, and staff.

Don't just include bios on your partners or worse, just the founder or founding partners. Include a picture and complete bio on every attorney and at least a short bio and picture of your staff. Depending on the size of your firm, you will want to feature a video introduction for each attorney. It's not necessary for staff, but do include it for each of the partners, attorneys, and if your budget can afford it, your associates as well.

Networking

People want to do business with their friends. Even though technology has advanced and communication happens in the blink of an eye and sometimes without our physically being a part of it, people still want to do business with people they know and trust. This is why networking is probably your most important sales tool and a foundational piece of your marketing plan.

Networking is a long-term tactic. While getting started this week may lead to a quick sale or new client, it's more likely that the results will come slowly at first and then be your main source of new business over the years. There's really no way to stress how important networking is for a professional, especially an attorney.

Think about your little black book. You probably keep it in the form of an MS Outlook, Gmail contact list, or an ACT database. Maybe you have an actual little black book. If you still have a little black book, you should consider joining the 21st century. However, use whatever format works for you, but treat this list as your most valuable business asset. If it isn't so today, it will be soon.

There are whole books written on networking, and we could take several chapters here. If you want to learn complex systems for networking and connecting, knock yourself out. However, here we'll try to boil it down into a manageable system for marketing success.

Before we start, here are a few ground rules:

Tell the truth. Don't be tempted to cover up or hide bad news or unflattering facts about you or your business. In the words of John Maxwell: "If you're lying, you're lying."

Keep your promises. If you say you'll get someone a piece of information or make a copy of an article, then do it. Create whatever system you need to keep up with your tasks, but do what you say you'll do.

Don't overpromise. The temptation is to promise big things to impress. Resist this temptation to overdeliver. Your contacts will be much more impressed with your exceeding their expectations than barely covering a big promise.

Be consistent. Develop a system that works for you and keep at it. Networking is a long-term strategy and will not deliver huge results overnight.

Networking Step 1: Organize Your Contact List

Start by organizing your address book into logical categories. In whatever system you are using, you can create categories or groups. Use category names something like this:

- Friends and Family
- Service Providers
- Business Acquaintances/Associates
- Clients
- Prospects

Create as many categories for friends, family, and service providers as you like. You might have categories for medical providers, such as dentists, doctors, pharmacists and so forth and maybe personal categories, such as your Sunday school class, softball team, bridge club, and whatever works for you. It's the last three, business acquaintances, clients and prospects that are the important categories. The labels you choose to name the categories are not important. Keep in mind that some contacts may be in more than one category.

Networking Step 2: Choose Your Personal Top 10 Lists

After organizing your contact list into categories or groups, look at the business acquaintances, clients, and prospects lists. From each of the three categories, make a list of the top 10 or 15 contacts from each list. By their names, identify what you would like these people to do for you and what you can do for them. Spend a little time researching how you can help these individuals. How can you make valuable connections for them or provide industry research that will improve their business? Maybe you can provide personal legal or financial tips to help them personally. Treat this list as you would prospective clients in terms of connection frequency. Make contact with them at least every other month, if not more often.

Networking Step 3: Start Making Connections

Set aside time each week to make contact with your connections. Make it a regular part of your business day or week. This activity is as important as any you'll do to promote your firm and drive in new business.

Business Associates, Three Times per Year: Business associates are the bulk of your professional address book. These are your contacts from the different worlds of business: insurance, banking, professionals, other attorneys, chamber of commerce, industry, and other businesses. Make contact with these people at least three times per year. If you have 100 business associate contacts at three contacts per year, that's 300 contacts. If you use 50 weeks per year to do networking, that's six contacts from this group per week ($300 \div 50 = 6$). That's not so bad.

Clients, Four Times per Year: Clients should be contacted at least four times per year. These are the people who are currently putting food on your table. You need to keep developing their business, find new ways to provide value to these contacts, and hopefully get them to refer new business to you or your firm.

Prospects, Six Times per Year: Prospects need a little more care than the other groups. These are the people you hope will do business with you or your firm in the future. If you have a connection with these individuals already, then you can just contact them. If you don't have a personal connection, then start working your current connections and find out who can help you with an introduction. That becomes the real value of your database. Networking sites such as LinkedIn offer a valuable insight into who knows whom.

Learn about the business needs of this group. Spend a little time researching their businesses and their industries. Try to find ways to meet their needs and make their business life better. Maybe it's a connection they need to a new supplier or potential customer. It may be a piece of research you think will be valuable to their firm. And while you never want to improperly disclose proprietary information, maybe it's a piece of competitive information that will adversely affect their business if it remains unknown to the contact. The object is to provide value before asking for their business. If you provide value, they will want to find ways to repay the favor.

Networking Step 4: Types of Connections

There are dozens of ways to make contact with your connections. Feel free to be creative and use unusual contact methods. Mix up the order. Don't always phone or always send an e-mail. Use all different kinds of contacts. Customize your activity based on the contact and what's appropriate for each. You will need to create some sort of database for keeping track of when to contact each and any information that was revealed in the last contact. A contact or customer database management software program is ideal for this activity since you can schedule your next contact date and keep track of information and tasks.

Phone: This involves picking up the phone, dialing the contact's phone number, and having a chat. Be prepared, if possible, to provide some industry information, share some business knowledge, offer to make a connection, or just ask about family and business. Find out what's new and ask whether there's anything you can do. In many cases, you're just going to stay connected with a short chat.

E-mail: Send a personal e-mail. Adding your contacts to an automated mailing list for your company newsletter does not count as a personal e-mail. Remember, the object is to connect on a personal level with your contact.

Personal Note: A personal, handwritten note is an excellent way to make contact with your list. Send a congratulatory note for a personal accomplishment or mention in the local newspaper. Clip a news story and include it with your note about an industry happening, as well as a civic or charitable event. Personal note cards can be formal with your name or initial printed or a card with a special illustration, photograph, or other design. You'll want to use cards that are blank inside so you have plenty of room to write a personal note. We rarely get personal notes in the mail these days, which makes this one of our favorite connections.

Event Card: An event card is a birthday, marriage, anniversary, get well, graduation, or other type of greeting card with a preprinted message designed by Hallmark or other greeting card company. Using event cards is fine as long as you use them only occasionally and you write a personal note on the inside. And by personal note, we mean something other than, "I hope you have a nice birthday!"

Face-to-Face Meeting: A face-to-face meeting can take several different forms. The form you use isn't as important as the face-to-face part. You can invite the contact for a meal, such as breakfast or lunch, or for a beverage, such as coffee or a happy hour cocktail. Not all business people drink alcohol, and you should limit your consumption so as to remain sharp. Remember, while this meeting is over a meal or in a coffee shop, you are conducting serious business.

Special Event: A special event might involve sports, such as a football or baseball game, or a cultural outing, such as a play or concert. These type connections tend to be expensive, so be careful how you use them.

Networking, as we've used it here, is a little different from attending networking events. Various organizations, such as the local chamber of commerce, BNI chapters, and other business-related groups, have regular networking events. Local business people are invited to meet at a restaurant or coffee shop to share a cocktail or coffee and chat about business. These events may be a valuable source of good business contacts. However, you have to guard your time and evaluate the kinds of business people who are attending and whether these contacts are valuable. It's easy to spend many hours each week at networking events with the wrong kinds of business people. If these are your kind of contacts, then by all means, attend and network with them. Once you make good connections at this type event, plug them into your address book formula for regular follow-ups.

Phase 2 Tactics

Phase 2 Tactics are the medium priority tactics. Start putting these tactics into practice as appropriate after you have all the Phase 1 Tactics in place.

Social Media

Social media have exploded in recent years. There are hundreds of millions of users on Facebook, LinkedIn, Twitter, Google+, and other social media platforms. The real question for you is whether your target audience is using social media, and if so, which ones. If they are, then you should be there as well. If you believe that your target audience is using primarily Facebook, for example, then you should create a Facebook business page. In some cases, businesses are using their Facebook page as their only web presence. I do not recommend that you do that for your law practice.

As of the beginning of 2012, we believe the following social media platforms make sense for most attorneys. Again, depending on your branding and your target clients, you'll make selections for participation in social media. Don't just jump in and join them all and start participating. Make the particular social media participation decisions based on your overall strategy and your resources.

You can get assistance in managing your social media presence from an administrative assistant, outsourced company, or even a paid consultant. However, you will still have to have some interaction with the platform if you hope to get the most benefit from your efforts. The focus of social medial is the social part. That means you'll have to find time to engage in some way.

LinkedIn

For a professional, start your social media experience with LinkedIn. LinkedIn is a social media site for professional networking. You can create a profile with resume type information but also list activities, accomplishments, summary information, specialties, skills, group memberships, and even blog feeds. You can join groups of like-minded professionals, share presentations, make connections to others, and even share your personal side with reading lists and blog feeds. Many people will use LinkedIn as their first source of information when looking for another professional. You can customize your profile, using keywords to promote yourself in certain areas of practice or geography.

Unlike many social media sites, LinkedIn is intuitive in terms of how to interact with others. By joining community, industry, or professional groups, you can join in on conversations, answer questions, research a topic, or just act socially. We think LinkedIn makes sense for all attorneys. Whether you participate heavily or not, you should have an up-to-date profile and be available to be found. Once you've used LinkedIn for a while, you'll start to understand how to use it to promote yourself or your firm. For starters, follow these steps:

Create a Profile: Create a complete profile. Use your keywords to highlight your experience, summary, and specialties. Your title should specifically highlight the key areas you want to promote. List the keyword areas separated by a "|" symbol. Include a professional looking headshot. Complete the skills section by selecting the skills that you possess and want to display. If you have publications, such as white papers or books, list them in the publications section. If you like, include your reading list populated with what you're reading now. In every section appropriate, list your phone number and e-mail. LinkedIn is not the place to be shy. Do you want people to contact you or not?

Make connections: Start by looking for people you are already know. Send a connection request with a short personal note asking for a connection. Don't use the generic LinkedIn request.

Join groups: Browse the groups function and select groups from your industry, specialty, or interests. Some groups are open, which means anyone can join. Some are locked, which means you have to be approved. When you apply to join, send the moderator a short note explaining why you want to join, and you will likely be approved quickly. Unless you're going to be a power user, set your e-mail preferences to weekly settings, or you will quickly be inundated with e-mail updates that you really don't want.

Get recommendations: Ask clients, former partners, and associates to give you a recommendation. Don't go overboard. In the beginning, three to five will be sufficient. As you continue to use LinkedIn, ask for additional recommendations as you do work for new clients.

Join the conversation: Browse the groups you've joined and engage in some of the comment threads. Many groups have an "introduce yourself" thread where you can make a quick introduction and say hello. Look through the group threads, and join the conversation where you have something to add.

Twitter

Twitter is a social media and micro blogging service that allows you to send text-based messages of no more than 140 characters. These messages are known as "tweets." Twitter tends to attract an older audience than other social media platforms, although that trend is starting to normalize.

To get started with Twitter, create an account, and populate your profile. Your Twitter account is a personal account, although many people try to make it a business account. It works best as a personal account. You can micro blog about your profession and personal interests. There are tools to help automate the regular posting process, such as HootSuite and TweetDeck. These tools allow you to schedule posts based on the calendar and time of day and take much of the burden out of regular posting.

You can search for people to follow by searching for specific names or topics. You can also search by hashtag. A hashtag is a "#" sign followed by a phrase. For example, "#legal" will give you a listing of individual posts that include that hashtag. Anyone can create a hashtag or use an existing one in their posts. The hashtag is a way to filter through some of the smoke to get to people who post about topics in which you are interested.

When creating your own posts, try to get a mix of conversation with other tweeters, information about your profession, news that affects your followers, and self-promotion. If you only self-promote, no one will care to follow you. Self-promotion should be no more than 20% to 30% of your posts. The most important posts will be conversations with others. Retweet posts that you find especially interesting, send messages to others, or respond to comments others make. Similar to how LinkedIn works, it's this conversation that really gets people interested and invested in you.

Facebook for Business

Facebook recently updated its business page function. You can now create a Facebook page for your law practice with timelines and custom layouts. While some of this functionality will likely require technical help, it is available and why some consumer-based businesses are choosing to build Facebook pages and no Internet website. Again, as an attorney, you should not duplicate this strategy. You need a separate Internet presence outside of Facebook.

With Facebook, you can post updates, link to Internet sites, and share news and pictures. You can allow several employees to have update authority to make management less burdensome. Most people understand how Facebook works. The new business pages make this a more interesting option than in the past.

YouTube

If you have created videos, you should have a YouTube account. There are other sites that will host a video and allow you to link to your website, but YouTube is the standard. If you haven't created any videos, what are you waiting for? Look for more information on using video in the "Video" section that follows.

Google+

This is just getting started and has not become a standard like the search engine. It operates as a cross between Facebook and LinkedIn. Only time will tell if this medium thrives or dies.

Blogs

Many attorneys are excellent writers. If you have some basic skills in this area, perhaps you can write a blog or articles. A blog is an on-line journal where you can write on business specific, personal, or general topics of interest. If you hope to promote your firm or yourself as an attorney, make sure the blog topics have some relevance to your practice. That's not to say that you should limit your topics to business topics. You can veer off the business trail from time to time on topics that are of particular interest to you. If you are involved in a local civic club or charity, you can write blog entries about your group's activities and causes. If you're trying to promote your firm, you must keep your brand in mind as you select topics.

Managing a blog and creating posts to promote your firm require a plan. Think about the topics you want to cover, the frequency of your posts, and the effect that the calendar has on your practice. You should be consistent in your posting. If you want to post once a week, make it the same day, once a week. If you want to post a few times a week, then be consistent in doing that. You may want to write on a different topic each month. Perhaps you want a schedule of progression on a topic. Start at the logical beginning of the issues, and gradually expand in a linear fashion over a period of time. A completely random topic list based on news of the day and how it affects your clientele might work as well.

As with a website, you'll be more successful if you write about topics that people find interesting and if you use appropriate keywords for that topic. When we say "interesting," we mean interesting within the general topic area and to your target audience. You may be writing on some scientific topic that does not interest the general public at all. But you aren't writing for the general public; you're writing for your target audience—that is, your customers. Your articles must be interesting and topical to this group of people.

Article Writing

If you're a decent writer, but don't have the dedication to write a blog every few days or weekly, then perhaps you can write articles about your particular area of interest. An article in an industry journal can be used to promote your firm and increase your professionalism. In addition to magazines and journals for your particular legal practice areas, you can contribute articles to industry journals related to the areas in which you practice. If you work with companies in the energy business, you could contribute articles to *Oil & Gas Journal, Offshore Magazine, Oil and Gas Investor,* and so forth. Practically every industry in business has a trade journal or magazine.

In addition to industry magazines and professional journals, you can publish articles to article marketing websites. Two of the biggest websites that promote articles are EzineArticles.com and GoArticles.com. You can create an account and submit articles about any topic you choose. Each site has publishing guidelines, but it's generally easy to comply. These sites then submit your articles to portals and information services, overdriving traffic to your article. With each article, you include a bio that will have a link back to your website. The key to a successful article writing campaign is similar to promoting a website or blog. Write articles that are interesting, use keywords for the topic, and provide good content.

Public Speaking

In every community, there are many opportunities for public speaking, and you probably don't have to look very hard for them either. There are civic clubs, such as the Rotary Club and the Civitan Club, that have organizations in most towns across the country. These groups meet either weekly or monthly and have a presentation as part of their regular meeting. They are always looking for speakers on interesting topics that are appropriate for their club members. Just contact the club and find out who handles the speaker scheduling. There are other clubs available. In many communities, the Sunday newspaper will list club meetings for the next week or will have a monthly listing.

In addition to civic groups, the public library in many communities offers free workshops for the public on topics from Microsoft Office applications to creative writing. Contact the library to see what they offer and whether you can add a topic to their schedule. If your library doesn't offer these types of free workshops, perhaps your firm can sponsor the series and handle the scheduling as a public service to the community and the library.

Volunteer or ask to be a speaker at industry group meetings. You and other attorneys in your firm probably do regular work in certain industries. Investigate the industry associations and look for opportunities to speak to groups of industry participants. This will not only set you up as an expert but will also allow you to market to a group of potential clients.

If you are afraid to speak publicly, then join a local chapter of Toastmasters International. They have chapters in many communities and provide a place to learn the skills necessary to speak well and a forum to practice these skills. Don't use an excuse not to be able to speak to a group. You're an attorney. You made it through college and law school. You can do this. Not being able to give a talk to a group of people because you are afraid is just unacceptable.

Workshops

In addition to speaking to and for groups, you can sponsor your own workshops for professionals or the public. Depending on your area of practice, you can develop workshops on topics of interest to different groups. These can be free or paid workshops. Again, like any other marketing tactic, make sure that what you're doing supports your brand.

Many firms use workshops to generate new business. If you're in the elder law practice, you could offer workshops on Social Security benefits, estate planning, or family trusts to give people basic information on the particular topic and generate new clients. Make sure to give good content in the workshop. Don't just offer a teaser workshop in the hopes of getting people to hire your firm. If you don't give workshop attendees good content in the first place, they're unlikely to want to hire your firm.

In addition to landing new clients from the workshop, the act of presenting the topic will hopefully increase awareness of your firm and you as an attorney while improving your reputation in the community.

After the workshop, send an e-mail to all attendees, thanking them for attending. Follow up with any after seminar requests, distribute handouts you promised, and take an opportunity to ask for their business.

Videos

We discussed the use of videos on your website earlier. You may want to go beyond just attorney introductions on bio pages and spread a few well-placed topical videos around your site. You might choose to create a whole program of educational videos for use by your customers. If the content is especially valuable, you might consider creating a paid content site for marketing on the Internet. Consumers will pay for valuable content, especially if paying a small fee to you will save them hundreds or thousands of dollars they would have to spend hiring their own attorney.

Depending on your branding and practice area, you could create video content, introduction content, and teaser content to promote other video products, e-books, blogs, or just your website. You can make easy and inexpensive videos from your laptop video camera or hire a professional video firm to create a professional product. Again, as with all the tactics in this book, you need to consider your brand and what is appropriate for the image you are trying to promote for your firm.

This area of video is loaded with options to promote your firm and attorneys. Rather than talking in generalities, I'll give three examples to illustrate the point.

Example 1: Corporate Bankruptcy. You could create a series of videos to educate your customers on how the corporate bankruptcy law works including:

- What can you expect from a bankruptcy?
- What action do you take if your customer declares bankruptcy, owing you money?
- What is a creditor's committee all about?
- Can we accept this check for payment of an old invoice?
- Can we continue selling to our customer who declared bankruptcy?

There are literally dozens, if not hundreds, of topics that could be covered from both sides of the bankruptcy filing. The firm going through a bankruptcy filing needs certain information as does the firm whose customers are going through bankruptcy.

Example 2: Elder Law. You could create video designed for seniors and their adult children to address:

- Using a family trust to protect family assets.
- Dealing with nursing home abuse.
- Creating an estate plan.
- Curbing the power of attorney abuse.

- Understanding Social Security benefits for spouses.

Example 3: Mergers and Acquisitions. Your firm represents clients who buy or acquire other companies. You could create videos to educate your clients about:

- The value of a company.
- Types of valuation models.
- The value of obsolete inventory.
- Cash flow versus income models.
- Due diligence process.

As you can see from these three examples, we've just touched on the possibilities. As experts in these and hundreds of different practice areas, your firm can position itself as an expert by creating educational videos to provide basic education, creating paid content, or merely getting traffic to your website. Always keep in mind your brand, the purpose of your on-line presence, and your firm's marketing goals and objectives. In other words, have a plan first, and then create the content.

Charity/Civic/Community Activities

We covered this item in the previous chapter. Select appropriate charitable organizations, civic groups, or community activities in which you and your staff can participate. This type of work promotes your firm and gives you a boost in credibility.

Guerrilla Tactics

The specific tactics listed in the three categories are those tactics that will apply to most law firms. The following list is based on the idea of "guerilla" tactics, as in *Guerilla Marketing*, the 1984 book by Jay Conrad Levinson. The term "guerilla" refers to unconventional and often cheap or free approaches. This list of guerilla tactics is more of a creativity jogger than an actual game plan. Think about how you can use unconventional methods that complement your brand and overall marketing goals to promote your firm. Here are a few to get you thinking.

Donate magazine subscriptions to nursing homes, schools, and jails, leaving your address label attached.

Use a welcome sign in your lobby, and list client names that have appointments. This is a small effort that makes a big impression. Everyone likes to see his or her name in a place of prominence.

Never leave a potential client meeting without identifying the next steps. Don't leave the meeting thinking that the potential client will call any day and ask to do business with you. Identify the next steps towards doing business together while everyone is sitting around the table.

Always be early to seminars, meetings, and conferences. You can choose with whom you will meet and network and whom you'll sit next to. If you're late, you don't get to choose to sit next to a potentially important client, and you lose valuable networking time.

Phase 3 Tactics

Phase 3 Tactics are the organized advertising tactics. It's not that they aren't important, but we realize that you can't do everything at once. After you have put together a plan and implemented the Phase 1 tactics and the appropriate Phase 2 tactics, you can start thinking about your growth goals and your investment in organized advertising.

For professionals, and especially attorneys, the object of organized advertising is to increase brand awareness. Your service is unlike selling burgers and sneakers. There typically isn't an immediate need. You're hoping your potential clients are exposed to your tactic and remember your branding when it's time to make the decision, usually at a later time.

Organized advertising tends to be fairly expensive compared to many of the other tactics that require more time than money. A poorly planned advertising tactic will allow a small business to throw away a bunch of cash in a short period of time with nothing to show for it. If you don't have any experience in these media, get some help. Don't let a sales rep for a TV or radio station sell you on a program of advertising without a solid plan in mind. A solid plan requires you to identify a specific goal, a budget, and a target audience before you start listening to the pitch. After the pitch, you'll need to develop with the rep which metrics you'll use for measuring success. If you go in blind, you'll get robbed blind. Media sales reps are there to sell their advertising. If you don't have a specific plan, budget, and target audience in mind, they'll set you up with whatever they have the most of to sell. It's not that these folks are crooks or dishonest. They are selling a product. It's up to you to make sure it's right for your business, just like buying any other product for your business. You wouldn't go into an equipment acquisition without knowing specifically what the equipment needed to do and a well-established budget. You wouldn't even consider just buying a random piece of equipment and telling the sales rep to give you something to make products with. You'd end up with waffle irons in a machine shop.

Organized advertising is no different from any other marketing tactic in that you need to have a plan, a budget, and a target audience. We're not saying don't do media buys.

We're saying to get help if you need help, do your homework, and go in with your eyes open if you're going to do it yourself.

Consider the time of year or season when choosing your options. Some tactics work better at one time of year than another. For example, more people go to movie theaters during the winter and especially around the Christmas holidays than at other times of the year. Not all tactics are seasonal, so it's best to plan carefully.

In most of the media discussed here, you will get a better price per ad by agreeing to a long-term agreement. Many times you'll get your agreed-to spots plus some free spots for signing a long-term contract.

Our experience suggests that attorneys do best when they combine multiple advertising tactics. An example would be combining a print ad with a 30-second announcement promoting an upcoming fund-raiser sponsored by the law firm. These types of combinations give you good exposure to the market, plus the law firm gets some credibility transfer from the charity.

Print

Print advertising is what most people think of as an advertising tactic. Print advertising includes tactics, such as newspapers, magazines, billboards, transit banners (buses), vehicle wraps, movie theater preshow ads, school yearbook and event ads, and charity logo goodwill partnerships.

Start looking at print options based on the demographic of your target clients. What publications do they typically read, buy, or subscribe to? Start with the customers and work backwards. Find out where they spend their time, and you'll discover where you should be presenting your brand and message.

Speak with the publication sales staff, and make sure your ad will not be placed next to a competitor's or in an undesirable location within the publication. You can use your own graphic artist or one from the publication. If you have very specific requirements for your ad, use your own people.

Start small, and measure effectiveness. Don't blow your entire budget on a single ad or spot. If you pay attention, you'll learn the ropes quickly. Don't pull your ad if you don't get an immediate response. It often takes multiple views by a customer to change behavior.

Internet

Internet advertising tactics include such things as banner or tile ads on other websites, search engine keyword advertising, and preference advertising. Preference advertising happens when you are looking at products on Amazon.com, for example, and then browse another website where Amazon advertises. You'll probably notice that the product being advertised is the product you were just looking at on Amazon. While this can be a little off-putting in a big-brother kind of way for the customer, it does directly relate to what you were searching for on another site.

The Internet works just like the other forms of organized advertising in that it is priced based on the number of people who are attracted to the site. A website that attracts 100 visitors per day will be significantly less expensive than a site that attracts 10,000 visitors per day. Again, it's all about finding your target audience. It really doesn't matter how many visitors per day a site attracts if they aren't your target. A website with 100,000 people per day searching for waffle irons is not going to be a good place to advertise industrial equipment.

Radio/TV

Radio and TV advertising tactics include audio advertisement (radio) and video commercials (TV), program sponsorships, and paid program slots for both radio and TV.

Radio and TV spots require repetition for maximum effectiveness. Running an ad a few times a week will not be nearly as effective as running it several times a day. Media rules of thumb suggest it takes six repetitions before gaining brand awareness. Are you prepared to run your spot frequently over several weeks or months to gain the brand recall that translates into business? And remember, it's not the number of times you run the ad that is important. It's the number of times your ad is heard by your target that is the important point. In a law firm setting, advertising with radio and TV can be quite productive. However, our experience suggests that creating brand recall over the long term should be the appropriate goal, not trying to generate immediate ROI. Additionally, we have found that professionals achieve more success by combining a radio or TV spot with a form of print, such as billboards, transit banners, or print ads. The combination of approaches helps to increase the number of people in a target population that are exposed to the ad (reach) and the number of times a person sees or hears that ad (frequency).

Many radio stations now stream their content live on the Internet, multiplying the number of advertising options available. Local National Public Radio (NPR) stations offer program or day sponsors that often make good advertising tactics, if your target audience matches that of the station. For many attorneys, this is a good match, but don't take our word for it; check out the station demographics at different time slots.

Attorney Treasure Chest

The Attorney Treasure Chest is a compilation of interesting tactics that any firm can add to its marketing plan. Feel free to use these items as is or modify them to fit your particular firm. All of these tactics will not be right for your firm. Remember that any marketing tactic you use must support your brand.

Chamber of Commerce: Join the local chamber, attend networking events, and get involved in committees and ambassador programs. Volunteer to lead workshops and classes that benefit the general chamber membership.

Newspaper: Introduce yourself to the editorial staff of the local newspaper. You should know the news editor and the business editor at a minimum. In larger papers, there may be additional sections that relate to your practice area. When industry news breaks nationally, be sure to send them links or a heads up. Offer your interpretation of the events and offer to translate the legalese into plain English for their readership. Offer to write articles on issues that affect their readership.

Business Cards: In addition to the previous discussion about business cards, you can also post them on bulletin boards at community centers and grocery stores, and leave a card on the table whenever you dine out. Be sure to give cards to the wait staff at your favorite restaurants, and make sure they know you're an attorney and the areas in which you practice. Encourage them to hand out your cards to others.

Name Tags: Always wear a name tag when attending events. Wear it on your right lapel so it's readily visible when shaking hands. A name tag is a portable billboard that helps people remember your name and the name of your firm. Your local printer can create a professional name tag with your branding that includes a magnetic attachment so as not to ruin silk blouses or suit coats. Have name tags printed for your employees that function in the community. If any of your staff attend chamber of commerce functions, charity or civic clubs, or networking events on their own behalf, make sure they have a proper name tag with your firm's branding.

Signature Block: Add a signature block to your outgoing e-mail that is appropriately branded and lists your firm name, address, and other contact information. Make sure every firm employee uses this e-mail signature branding for their business correspondence.

Greeting Cards: Send birthday and anniversary cards to clients and colleagues. Special life events, such as graduations, deaths, births, and marriages, are also great opportunities for you to connect with people you know. Instead of the standard Christmas or holiday card at year-end, send a Thanksgiving card in November. The early arrival of a "holiday" card will be unique and tend to stay around longer to remind your connections you're thinking of them. The uniqueness of the Thanksgiving card makes it memorable.

Volunteer: Donate your time and that of your employees to local civic and charitable groups and city/county boards.

These boards and clubs tend to get publicity and show you and your firm as givers.

Press Releases: Use press releases whenever possible to promote the activities of your firm. You can highlight new hires, new offices, big cases, your selection as the representative for a group, or special activities in which your firm participates. The press release must be in the proper format and read like a news story. Use news industry formatting of tight sentences and short paragraphs as you answer the "who, what, when, where, and why" questions. If you don't know how to format or write a press release, get help from your marketing firm. They will also have the contact information in place for newspapers, magazines, TV, and radio connections to help get added publicity.

Newsletter: Create and write a firm newsletter. Send the newsletter out via e-mail to firm clients and partners. Create a big, splashy first edition, and give all your other contacts an opportunity to receive the list. Use the newsletter to share information about legal trends, highlight employees, discuss important issues facing your clients, and explain complicated legal concepts that come up in normal conversations with your clients.

HELP! Cards: Create laminated or heavy stock cards with information about what to do in case of an accident, DUI, arrest, burglary, or other incident appropriate to your line of practice.

Newsletter Advertisement: Advertise or sponsor the newsletter for a church, school, or community group. These newsletters tend to be very well read and give you an opportunity to get your firm name in front of people associated with that group. Pick groups or schools that best fit your marketing goals and brand.

Google Places: Own your firm's listing, and complete the free profile for Google, Yahoo!, Bing, and AOL. When someone does an Internet search for "attorney hometown," you want to show up in the first few references. Consider your keywords as you complete the free profile for these services. Many firms either have no listing or are using the search engine default listing. An owner-completed listing will be moved up in the ranking ahead of the default listings. In some cases, you may be the only claimed listing for a community.

Directories: Participate in any free directories that are appropriate.

Never Eat Alone: Use breakfast and lunch meals as an opportunity to network. Keith Ferrazzi wrote a whole book on the topic. Don't go to lunch every day with your office colleagues or worse, by yourself. Take one or two days a week to invite a prospective client or network contact to lunch. Use this valuable time to make yourself more valuable.

Billing Statements: First and foremost, make sure that your billing statements are accurate. Take a hard look at the format of your statements, and determine whether a change of format might make them easier to understand. Make sure to use descriptive and specific language to describe the services you rendered. Don't use terms such as "for services rendered" or the like when a specific descriptive term could be used. These catch-all phrases tend to upset clients who can't remember what you did in the first place.

Use your statement to cross-sell your practice by including a message in the footer of the statement to promote different services offered by your firm that might be interesting to your clients. You can also use the footer to promote a charitable organization your firm supports or a special event coming soon.

Google Alerts: Use the alerts function of the Google search engine to send you an e-mail when a particular topic is found on the Internet. Look for topics that affect the industries in which your clients work, your client names, your firm name, and so forth. This is a great way to get breaking news about industries or topics to use to keep connections informed or your favorite newspaper editor friendly.

Twitter Alerts: Like the Google Alerts function, TweetBeep.com has a Twitter alert feature that will alert you when someone tweets about a particular topic. You can set up the alert to meet your needs. Google and Twitter do not play well together (as of early 2012), so your Google Alert function will likely not alert you to Twitter feeds with your particular information needs.

Breaking News: When big things happen in your community or industries in which you practice, be prepared to get information out via your normal outlets to help people in need respond appropriately. Use your normal outlets, such as press releases, social media, blog posts, website, and video blog entries to get your information out to the affected groups. Use the opportunity to share needed information to help people respond to their particular needs. Do not use it as a means to blatantly promote your firm.

Breaking News Example: You participate in a large international trade group that does business in some foreign country. You get word of a political coup d'état that threatens employees and financial assets of group member companies deployed in the country. You could send out e-mail alerts, post blog entries, and send press releases to inform affected businesses about emergency contacts in the country where they can check on the welfare of their employees. You could also provide information relevant to protecting their physical and financial assets. This assumes that you have such information available. You might have to do a little research or make some calls to be able to provide accurate information.

Answer the #%@! phone: Americans regularly rank immediate availability as important in surveys affecting the selection of service providers. If you can't or don't want to answer the phone due to another issue, at least return the message the same day. Even if it means returning the call after business hours and leaving a message, the client will know you cared enough to call him or her back.

This is far from a complete list of marketing tactics. We're sure a little brainstorming in your firm will come up with a much better list appropriate for your firm's branding message. The key is to think about the needs of your clients and find ways to fulfill those needs in interesting or unusual ways.

Monitor

Not to be forgotten is the last step—monitoring. It is just as important as the other steps but frequently never happens. You've researched and planned and devised and scheduled, and now you're tired and just want to get to work. Your tactic takes place, and you start thinking about the next one without analyzing and documenting the results of the former tactic. Did you compare the actual results to your goal? If you don't monitor your activities, you'll never know whether they are working and whether to do more or do less of that particular activity.

A critical component of the monitoring is figuring out upfront how you will measure the success of each tactic. That should be a component of devising the goal. Make each goal specific and measurable. To suggest that you want to increase sales from a particular line of advertising is entirely too vague. We want to increase sales to 15% in the elder law services division of our firm in year one and to 25% by end of year two.

Once you have a specific and measurable goal, decide how you will actually measure. In most cases, this will be obvious and clear. But if you have two or more activities working at the same time, you need to spend a little time devising a way to tell from where the potential increase in business is coming. How will you know if new business is coming from a social media campaign or that newspaper ad you bought? Use special departments, phone numbers, and web splash pages to identify and segregate traffic so you have a method to measure the increased activity and identify from where it came.

As you get data from each tactic, compare what you did and how you did it to the results you got. Consider changing the copy, color, pricing, or layout to get different results. As you tweak your tactics, note the change in performance, and try to continually improve your results. When you hit on a great tactic, try to use it as a template for future tactics.

Summary

Creating a marketing plan can be a simple exercise if you follow the plan. Do your research to understand your industry, market segments, competition, and clients. With a critical eye, review your firm's strengths and weaknesses. Plan your strategy by identifying your unique sales proposition, brand, product pricing, distribution channels, and promotional goals. Create action plans to put your tactics to work. Finally, measure the results of your marketing activities, and make corrective action to improve your results.

See our other small business advisory books at www.BusinessStartup101.com or Amazon.com:

Business Start-up 101: From Great Idea to Profit…Quick!

Business Plan Template: How to Write a Business Plan

Marketing Plan Template: Writing Marketing Plans for Small Business

About the Authors

Chris Gattis

Chris started what is now Blue Point Strategies, LLC, a business consultancy, in 1984. He works with business owners who are struggling with the business part of running a business. From start-ups to turnarounds, Chris works with owners of small businesses to develop strategies and systems so they can achieve the financial success that drove them into business in the first place. Blue Point Strategies offers workshops, classes, consulting, and one-on-one coaching to assist business owners in achieving their dreams.

Chris has a background in corporate finance and operations, having served in various direct capacities, including CFO of the nation's largest privately-held insulation and construction products distributor; credit manager for the U.S. division of a multinational construction products manufacturer; and director of a small plastics manufacturing business. He has over 27 years of successful experience managing start-ups and turnarounds of large and small businesses as well as financial analysis, budget formulation, strategic planning, team building, and risk management. Chris has managed small businesses, wrestled with unreasonable demands from banks, and struggled with cash flow to make payroll. He understands the needs of and demands on small business owners.

His consulting experiences range from advising individual clients on real estate financing and development activities to managing start-ups and turnarounds of small businesses. He also has advised on site selection and expansion activities for a major Japanese automaker and various Tier 1 auto suppliers.

Chris has served on local planning and zoning commissions and development authorities, giving him keen insight into dealing with local cities and towns to further his clients' needs. In addition to his consulting practice, Chris serves as a business coach for local entrepreneurial development centers, an instructor for an area technical college, and a keynote speaker.

Blue Point Strategies, LLC
Huntsville, Alabama
www.BluePointStrategies.com
cgattis@BluePointStrategies.com

Felica Sparks

Felica Sparks of Ad4! Group has been a small business advocate since she was 8 years old. It was the desire to be responsible for her own allowance that inspired her to start her first business, a local lemonade stand. From running that lemonade stand to becoming a state vice president of Future Business Leaders of America as a junior in high school, Felica has always had the entrepreneurial spirit.

Felica's adult career started out in the financial arena. She worked in small local and regional banks in the Huntsville, Alabama, area. Working for the smaller banks gave her the freedom to be more of a hands-on partner with her commercial clients. It was from the desire to be a part of the commercial client's business growth that sparked her desire to become even more integrated in commercial development.

After 13 years in the financial industry, Felica joined one of her commercial clients and went into advertising and marketing at one of the larger Huntsville firms. Several years later, Felica got the entrepreneurial bug again and started the Ad4! Group. Since 2005, she has been concentrating on brand development and marketing strategies.

Ad4! Group
Huntsville, Alabama
www.ad4group.com
Felica@ad4group.com

www.BusinessStartup101.com